What People Are Saying

Having met Dr. Joe Rubino at his introduction to the Network Marketing industry, I have been privileged to witness his metamorphosis into leadership mastery. The key to Dr. Joe's wisdom is his being the consummate student. Through *The 7-Step Success System* we are the benefactors of his passion for research and marketing success.

> —Randell Anderson, Author,
> *High-Performance Networking*

I consider this book to be *the* Bible on how to become successful in network marketing. It outlines a proven, high-integrity, people-honoring approach that will lead to your success and that of your team. Study and follow these steps and you *will* be successful!

> — Richard Brooke, Network Marketing Visionary
> and Author, *Mach II Starring You*

Joe has created a wonderful book for anyone who wants to achieve greater success. It gives a sensible roadmap to effectively using networking to achieve your dreams and solves age-old challenges with real, modern, equitable solutions.

> —Romanus Wolter, Author, *Kick Start Your
> Dream Business,* Radio Host and Success Coach:
> *The Entrepreneur Magazine Show*

Dr. Rubino's *7-Step System to Building a $1,000,000 Network Marketing Dynasty* is a true gift to all who desire to build wealth from home. With this simple, detailed system any new distributor can take years off the learning curve and any already successful leader can now share a proven business-building and personal-development structure to support others to be successful.

—Bob Burg, Author, *Endless Referrals*

Dr. Joe Rubino's *7-Steps* outlines exactly what it takes to build an ultra-successful network marketing business. By following these steps, I replaced my 6-figure professional income after 18 months.

—Dr. Tom Ventullo, President, Visionary International Partnerships

He's done it again!! Joe Rubino is one of the world's top networkers and in this tremendous new book he lays a roadmap for success that anyone can follow. If you're serious about creating success in network marketing this is a "must read" book!

—Cliff Walker, Network Marketing Millionaire

In the network marketing profession, few books spell out exactly how to achieve top-level success in point-by-point detail. Fewer still are written by experts in the network marketing and personal development arenas who have actually achieved top success with integrity. Dr. Joe Rubino's "7-Step System" is such a book and offers readers a clear and powerful guide to achieve million-dollar earner status. I strongly suggest you apply this wisdom if you want to EARN $500 to $50,000/month.

—Capt. Dave Klaybor, President of www.PowerLineSystems.ws

THE 7 STEP SUCCESS SYSTEM TO BUILDING A $1,000,000 NETWORK MARKETING DYNASTY

THE 7 STEP SUCCESS SYSTEM TO BUILDING A
$1,000,000
NETWORK MARKETING DYNASTY

*How to Achieve
Financial Independence through
Network Marketing*

DR. JOE RUBINO

WILEY

John Wiley & Sons, Inc.

Published by John Wiley & Sons, Inc., Hoboken, New Jersey.
Published simultaneously in Canada.

For general information on our other products and services please contact our Customer Care Department within the United States at (800) 762-2974, outside the United States at (317) 572-3993 or fax (317) 572-4002.

Wiley also publishes its books in a variety of electronic formats. Some content that appears in print may not be available in electronic books. For more information about Wiley products, visit our web site at www.Wiley.com.

Library of Congress Cataloging-in-Publication Data:
Rubino, Joe.
   The 7-step success system to building a $1,000,000 network marketing dynasty : How to achieve financial independence through network marketing / Joe Rubino.
     p. cm.
   Includes index.
   ISBN 0-471-70319-2 (pbk.)
   1. Multilevel marketing. I. Title: Seven-step success system to building a $1,000,000 network marketing dynasty. II. Title.
HF5415.126.R826   2005
658.8'72—dc22   2004020459

Printed in the United States of America.

10 9 8 7 6 5 4 3 2 1

CONTENTS

CONTENTS

FOREWORD

Create a compelling vision, learn to prospect for distributors to accomplish your vision, train them for success, and develop them into leaders . . . well, that sounds like a plan.

So what does a dentist know about network marketing? Good question. A lot. Joe Rubino took the time to learn dentistry and became a successful dentist. He followed that same success pattern to learn how to become a network professional, a teacher, and a leader for his successful organization.

You don't become a successful dentist by signing an application and grabbing a drill, and you won't become a successful network marketing leader by simply purchasing a distributor kit.

Joe Rubino took the time, invested the effort, and learned the skills necessary to create this seven-step plan. All you have to do is to follow Joe's steps.

Pay close attention to the beginning of this book while Joe helps you create a real vision, one that you can work with, a vision that will motivate you to succeed. Too many people try to rise to the top without a "workable vision." Let Joe take you through the steps and make your vision something that will be part of your everyday life.

Using the same detailed steps, you will be taken through the complete seven steps of your plan to greatness. You won't have to fill in missing parts. Joe makes sure you won't be left scratching your head and thinking, "What's missing?"

You can easily modify the examples Joe shares for your business. Joe has been there, he has done it, and he shares what worked for him. Radio advertising? Long distance prospecting? Local niche prospecting? Joe shares what worked for him by using real life examples. That's what you want to hear. Facts from someone who did it, not theories from someone who drank a beer and wrote a book about his 10-day career.

Make sure you complete the entire book. Why? Because you will really see the big picture when Joe gets to leadership. Did you ever wonder what leaders do and say? How leaders react to criticism? And what leaders try to accomplish?

Well, find out as you complete your journey through the *The 7-Step Success System.*

Enjoy your journey.

Tom "Big Al" Schreiter
www.fortunenow.com

PREFACE

etwork marketing is simply defined as the movement of products or services from the manufacturer to the ultimate consumer through a network of independent distributors. Whether they realize it or not, most people are already involved in some form of network marketing on a daily basis. For example, if a new restaurant opens in your town and you try it and like it, you are sure to recommend it to your friends. Because of your endorsement, your friends decide to visit the restaurant, which then benefits from your word-of-mouth recommendation. Your enthusiastic referral has resulted in an increase in business for the restaurant. Similarly, when you see a good movie, you tell others, who decide to see it because of your suggestion. In so many areas of our daily lives, we recommend products and services we like to others. The manufacturer or owner of these products and services benefits as a result of this behavior. The only difference between this casual recommending and formalized network marketing is that network marketing companies actually pay their independent associates for recommending the products and services they gladly share with others because of their satisfaction with them.

More than $85 billion worth of goods and services are distributed each year worldwide via the structure of Direct Selling, in which the representatives who offer these products to others are paid through compensation plans based upon network marketing. Network marketing products are known for being unique, of the highest quality, and backed by a money-back guarantee. There are literally thousands of products and services successfully recommended to millions of satisfied customers through the vehicle of network marketing. These products and services are too vast in nature for me to mention all that are offered but range from nutritional and weight loss products to pet-care, household, and personal care products to telephone and electric service to travel and health or legal insurance plans, to name just a few categories.

In America alone, someone new starts their own home-based network marketing business every 11 seconds. Fifty-five percent of Americans have purchased a network marketing product or service. More than 13 million people participated in network marketing sales in 2003. Each of these people wants the same thing: a step-by-step plan to show them how they can be successful in creating a life-changing income from home. This book speaks directly to this need.

Network marketing has often been called The People's Franchise because it allows almost anyone to get started in a business possessing the potential for extraordinary success with a small, low-risk investment. Indeed, the benefits of network marketing, in contrast to traditional franchising, are many:

- Low startup costs typically of a few hundred dollars compared to franchise fees typically ranging from $50,000 to $1 million or more
- No employees in contrast to the hassle of hiring, firing, and managing employees
- Flexible hours as opposed to a fixed, full-time retailer's schedule
- The ability to leverage your time and efforts by earning income from the efforts of many others

- Tremendous tax advantages allowing you to potentially write off your lifestyle
- Freedom of choice in determining with whom, where, and when you work
- Unlike traditional franchising, no need to pay royalties back to your parent company
- The potential for the creation of long-term residual income, allowing you to profit from the efforts of those you introduce, even if you should eventually opt to retire from actively building your business

However, in spite of the many benefits that network marketing offers, many, if not most who pursue a home-based business, struggle, suffer, and fail in their efforts to build significant wealth.

The reasons for these widespread failures and unrealized expectations are clear. With a traditional franchise, every single aspect of what to do is clearly spelled out for the franchise owner. For example, if you decided to spend a half-million dollars or more to purchase a McDonald's franchise, you'd receive specific training on every aspect of running your business. You'd follow a detailed layout for the setup of your restaurant. You'd be given a manual that teaches you what ingredients and amounts go into each menu item. You'd learn where the french-fry maker goes, what your employees need to wear, and what they say to customers. You'd be schooled in how to up-sell customers and how to greet and thank them for their patronage. Every aspect of running a successful McDonald's franchise would be laid out for all franchisees to follow exactly to the letter.

In contrast, most who become involved in network marketing do *not* approach their businesses by following the structure of a proven system that would dramatically increase their odds of success. They dabble or experiment. They speak to people when it's convenient to do so . . . and it rarely is! They treat their businesses more like a sometime hobby than the daily pursuit of a serious profession. And, most importantly, they lack a detailed support system to follow that would insure their success by allowing them to train others in this same successful methodology that they themselves follow. This book fills this need.

It does so by outlining the core seven steps or foundational areas that can allow anyone to duplicate the behaviors necessary to build a large, thriving network marketing business. All too often, distributors are left on their own to find a way to make their businesses work successfully. Many will not know how to generate sufficient qualified leads needed to stay in massive daily action. They might create a list of names but lack credibility with the prospects they approach. Maybe they'll dump information on others without first developing rapport or listening to what's important to their prospects. Perhaps they'll lack the enrollment skills to create value and effectively guide a conversation to a productive conclusion. They may lack a compelling vision. They may not be sufficiently self-motivated. They may fail to inspire others to step into a leadership role. There are literally a thousand pitfalls that can derail even the most excited new distributor's hopes and dreams, causing him to quit like the vast majority who tried network marketing but found that "no one wanted to do it."

Building an ultrasuccessful business goes beyond just learning what to say and do. It requires internalizing a number of critical foundational principles or distinctions. The extent to which a distributor possesses these distinctions will determine the level of wealth and accomplishment she will create in her business. These success principles are mastered through the process of consistent daily prospecting, follow-up, training, and coaching actions—in combination with an effective personal development program. This book provides those interested in acquiring these success distinctions with the specific tools essential for building a network marketing dynasty.

Like any other worthwhile training or personal development program, there is no arriving, only the continual process of learning, growing, and expanding in knowledge, wisdom, and effectiveness. This book is written to serve as a network marketing "bible" for both seasoned veterans and new, first-time distributors alike. The principles outlined apply equally to all companies and can serve as a duplicable road map leading to the creation of a solid, built-to-last organization that will increase in size and value over time: a network marketing dynasty.

Like any other successful undertaking, the first step in building your dynasty must start with visioning. By gaining clarity about your reasons for becoming involved, you'll be able to expound upon your initial goals to weave them into a compelling and inspirational vision. Such a vision will both motivate you to do the daily tasks necessary to bring about your success and inspire the future business partners you'll attract to create visions of their own. Powerful visions go well beyond goal setting. They fuel the positive expectations of success required to align actions with desires. Visions are the stuff that leadership is made of. Network marketing dynasties are created only by visionary leaders who breed other self-motivated visionary leaders who operate from a commitment to massive action until their dynasty is well-established and on autopilot.

All true visions inspire action. Without a plan that is consistent with realizing one's vision, the probability of manifesting these dreams is vastly diminished. A vision without consistent and persistent daily, grounded actions is not really a vision at all. It is only a nice idea that will soon evaporate into the ether, since it is based upon convenience rather than commitment.

Not only must any action plan be consistent (day in and day out) and persistent (until the job is done) but it must also be effective as well. It has been said that the definition of insanity is doing the same ineffective actions over and over and expecting a different result. All effective action plans are dynamic by nature. They adapt to regular feedback regarding what's working while continually evaluating what's missing, that if put into place, would generate the result desired. Effective network marketing plans take into account every important aspect of prospecting, follow-up, and training required in building a successful business.

The first and most critical of these disciplines is prospecting. Over-the-top success in this industry requires speaking with massive numbers of prospects—enough required to identify those individuals who will develop into on-fire, effective leaders. A successful plan will encompass how many people you will speak with, detail where you will obtain your prospects, clarify what you will say to them, and specify how you will support them in the evaluation, training, and eventually, the business-building process.

However, to build a true network marketing dynasty, just hitting the numbers alone is not enough. We must be effective in our conversations, adept at creating value, and genuinely interested in the success of the people with whom we will partner. Enrollment is the fine art that separates those who struggle, suffer, and fail, ineffective in their attempts to convince others of the value of their company's income opportunity from those who attract others with the magnetic charisma of a skilled enroller. Those who have mastered this art are seen as attractive business partners.

Enrollment success and the charismatic magnetism necessary to attract others into your business is not some mysterious or elusive gift that only a blessed few born leaders possess. It is a skilled and detailed art that can be learned by anyone willing to become a student of this discipline. I break down the components of a successful enrollment conversation so that you can both learn to become a master in the enrollment arts and be able to train and coach others to duplicate the same high levels of success you'll enjoy.

Success in network marketing is all about duplication. Once you've mastered enrollment, you'll want to create structures to support your organization to gain the necessary business-building distinctions. I outline a complete training structure that will support the education and championing of your distributors as they step into the position of being empowered, self-motivated leaders in massive action of their own. My training structure will facilitate building both at a local as well as a long-distance level. I discuss exactly how to groom your people to grow in their skills, confidence, and commitment levels, no matter where they live or what their prior experiences or levels of expertise.

Of course, your organization will grow only as rapidly as you do personally. Rather than focus just on training, I discuss exactly how you can create an effective personal development program to support your own growth and effectiveness and that of your team. You'll learn how to implement daily structures to identify where your personal effectiveness with others may be lacking. I outline a number of feedback programs to assist you to identify those elements that need further development to support the creation of your multimillion dollar organization. You'll discover the top 50 qualities that are critical to achieving top success in this business, and you'll be able to identify which of these qualities would most impact your own business growth. You'll learn the importance of listening to others, how to bring out the best in them, and to champion them to achieve levels of success that they hadn't dreamed possible.

Ultimately, you'll learn the secrets to effective leadership required to take your team to new heights. You'll uncover the strategies necessary to build leaders and learn how to lead this charge by example, as you inspire those around you with actions consistent with the leader you have declared yourself to be. In network marketing, our incomes are directly proportional to the numbers of inspired and inspirational leaders we develop. Building to the dynasty level will necessitate an effective structure for producing an unending stream of self-motivated leaders who eventually assume the prominent role you once held with your team. Each will learn to step into a prominent leadership role to build a successful team themselves while championing others to do the same. The difference between any person being just a distributor or declaring themselves to be a leader always begins with the decision to lead. When a distributor makes the decision to be a leader, she might regularly ask herself the question, "What actions are consistent with my decision to be a leader?" We'll explore more closely what this decision might look like, in Chapter 7.

When you commit to building your own dynasty by implementing these seven essential steps and training your team to duplicate your success by following the same system, you will have taken the mystery out of what is required to build a multimillion dollar network marketing organization. This book can serve as the turnkey system that will lead to your organization duplicating itself on purpose by following a proven program that works. By taking on the science of deliberately putting into place each of the elements essential to support achievement, you will have set the stage for others to do as you have done and to enjoy success of their own.

Have fun, enjoy the process, live long, and sponsor!

Yours in partnership and success,

—Dr. Joe Rubino

ACKNOWLEDGMENTS

This book is dedicated with sincere gratitude to my mentors. They are Richard Brooke, Randy Anderson, Ron Scheele, Mike Smith, and Carol McCall. My success as a network marketer would not have been possible without the contributions of these coaches and friends. Thank you for contributing to me and countless others the life-changing gift of personal empowerment through network marketing and personal development.

I also wish to acknowledge my long-time friend and business partner, Dr. Tom Ventullo. Tom and I entered this great opportunity of network marketing in 1991, retiring from our dental practice together, both at age 37. Tom taught me the meaning of partnership, being the first of tens of thousands of other partners who followed in our business. Our partnership continues to this day as co-founders of The Center for Personal Reinvention, www.CenterForPersonalReinvention.com, an organization committed to the excellence and success of others.

ABOUT THE AUTHOR

D r. Joe Rubino is an internationally acclaimed network marketing trainer, author, success coach, and the CEO of The Center for Personal Reinvention, an organization that provides personal and group coaching as well as productivity and leadership development courses. Dr. Joe retired from his successful million dollar dental practice at the age of 37, having replaced and exceeded his professional income with a network marketing residual income. He was featured on the cover of several leading publications including *Success Magazine* and in the cover story, "We Create Millionaires: How Network Marketing's Entrepreneurial Elite Are Building Fortunes at Breakneck Speed" because of his ability to champion others to succeed. Joe is the author of 7 international best-sellers, currently in 14 languages and 43 countries. They include:

- *Secrets of Building a Million Dollar Network Marketing Organization from a Guy Who's Been There, Done That and Shows You How You Can Do It, Too*
- *The Magic Lantern: A Fable about Leadership, Personal Excellence and Empowerment*
- *The Power to Succeed: 30 Principles for Maximizing Your Personal Effectiveness*
- *The Power to Succeed: More Principles for Powerful Living, Book II*
- *Restore Your Magnificence: A Life-Change Guide to Reclaiming Your Self-Esteem*

- *The Legend of the Light-Bearers: A Fable about Personal Reinvention and Global Transformation*
- *10 Weeks to Network Marketing Success: The Secrets to Launching Your Very Own Million-Dollar Organization in a 10-Week Business-Building and Personal-Development Self-Study Course*
- *Secret #1: Self-Motivation* Affirmation Tapes

Joe is now committed to supporting others to enjoy successful lives and businesses. His vision is to impact the lives of 20 million people to be prosperous and live without regrets. For information about The Center for Personal Reinvention and its services or to order any of Dr. Joe's books or tapes, visit www.CenterForPersonalReinvention.com. To contact Dr. Joe about the possibility of hiring him as your personal success coach, e-mail: DrJRubino@email.com or call 888-821-3135.

Introduction: The Promise
of Network Marketing

I s network marketing, or multilevel marketing (MLM) as it was often referred to in years past, a legitimate vehicle that most anyone can use to create wealth from home? Or is it instead a black hole of frustration whereby the vast majority who pursue its seductive promises of economic and time freedom attempt to build wealth to various extents but never actually achieve the levels of success that they once dreamed of attaining? The reality of the situation is that it can be both! The fact that some are able to realize vast success, amass great wealth, and live the so-often-promised "life of choice" while many others struggle and eventually quit with little to show for their efforts, is not typically the result of luck or of chance.

To the contrary, there are many good reasons for the realization of either outcome. Network marketing, like other skilled professions, is both an art and a science. There are solid, predictable reasons why some people succeed in achieving the promises of wealth, the satisfaction of fun and fulfilling work, and the treasured time freedom that this industry can offer, while others put out a valiant effort, only to fail.

This book outlines a detailed 7-Step System to take the mystery out of why some are able to amass life-changing wealth and live the lifestyle of their fondest dreams. It is no wonder why such achievers would see this industry as a means to fun and freedom. The 7-Step System that follows is the result of 14 years of personal experience in building a multimillion dollar network. It is a compilation of the training of dozens of top network marketing leaders and thousands of hours of learning firsthand what works and what does not.

If you might be thinking that the training and coaching tips that follow are only effective for the elite, superbly gifted individuals, allow me to dispel this myth by sharing my story. I was first introduced to network marketing in 1991 when I answered a classified advertisement in a niche magazine. At the time, I was what most would consider a very successful dentist, earning a high six-figure yearly income. The problem I wrestled with was not the money. It was the stress, the physically demanding nature of the job (my neck and back problems were constant) and the responsibility of managing a team of 15 dental professionals. I didn't just own my business; my business owned me. Time freedom was something only others enjoyed.

So when I first learned of the possibilities that network marketing provided in terms of replacing my earned income with a residual income that would allow me the time freedom to do what I wanted to do, when I wanted to do it, the notion of walking away from the stresses and challenges of owning and operating a large dental practice was quite appealing. There was one small challenge. I was a shy introverted dentist with poor rapport building and communications skills and no clue regarding what it would take to build a million dollar network marketing dynasty. And I was scared to death to speak with people! Like so many others, I was afraid to approach my friends and family, fearing that they wouldn't like me if I prospected them or they might take offense to my boldness in trying to get them to do something that they had no interest in doing. But what was even more frightening to me was the prospect of having to speak with strangers. In short, I was not exactly the type of person you'd bet the family fortune on if you had to predict my success in this arena. In fact, one of my mentors, Randy Anderson, still takes pride in telling large audiences how I couldn't successfully lead three people in silent prayer!

So how could one with such overwhelming fears and deficiencies not only learn how to become successful in network marketing but also actually hope to teach and inspire others to become successful? The answer was to break down every element that would be needed to achieve success, to undertake a rigorous program of personal development, and to learn it so well that I could teach it to others to duplicate. I believed that if I could become successful in an industry where effective communication, relationship building, and leadership principles were so important, then so could just about anyone else who was equally committed to studying the same foundational principles while applying them daily in building a networking dynasty.

My study of what it takes to be effective in building a large networking organization continues to this day. In some areas, I've become quite proficient, while in others, I remain a self-declared neophyte. As you will read in the pages that follow, I have learned that success in this industry results from mastery of seven different yet related disciplines. Master these seven and you *will* be successful. Of course, these steps to success are all predicated upon two core principles we explore in great detail:

1. Massive, consistent, and persistent action
2. Working on your personal effectiveness with others on a daily basis

We must formulate the habit of continually looking at what's working in our business and in our personal communication. At the same time, we must also look for what might be missing, that if put into place, would better support our productivity and personal effectiveness. By doing so, we

xxviii INTRODUCTION

can't help but fuel the engine of constant and never-ending improvement.

Our industry boasts a considerable number who earn up to $1 million per year while a few individuals earn this same staggering sum each and every month! Of course, there are many more networkers who earn between $1,000 and $10,000 per month. However, the vast majority who start a network marketing business quit before reaching the levels of success they once hoped to attain upon joining. As a rule, these people typically lack the motivation, effort, training, and personal effectiveness skills to achieve the incomes they want. Like ones in other respected professions, those who lack sufficient ambition or seriousness in the pursuit of their business building are destined to give up before sponsoring that ace who will go on to build a lasting networking dynasty. The good news is that anyone possessing the self-motivation to stay in action for the long term while willing to be coached to build an ultrasuccessful business can be taught to do so. It requires committing to a consistent effort in following the 7-Step System outlined in this book while becoming a perpetual student of this great profession. Before we look at these steps to success in greater detail, let's examine the vehicle that makes this success possible — the network marketing concept.

Network marketing was first pioneered in the United States more than 50 years ago. It is a form of direct selling formulated around the concept of developing satisfied customers who are happy to share their enthusiasm for products they like (as well as for an income opportunity that results from marketing these superior products) with others who likewise do the same. Network marketers are typically not professional salespeople. Most are not full-time or even part-time, but *some-time* independent representatives who do not like to sell at all. Though network marketers are encouraged to sell their products or services, there are no quotas and no exclusive territories. It is, in fact, possible to be extremely successful in this business by simply using the products personally, recommending them (along with the income opportunity) to others, and sponsoring those interested in earning an income. One need not necessarily sponsor a lot of business builders to be quite successful. Many who earn $10,000 or more monthly in network marketing have sponsored only four to six leaders who have gone on to sponsor a handful of others. Success builds as a lot of people use their company's products daily and sponsor a few other like-minded entrepreneurs who duplicate this same behavior.

In network marketing, fortunes are created in a manner similar to the concept of compounding interest, based upon the doubling effect. Successful representatives sponsor a few other representatives who sponsor a few others and so on. As the numbers of each subsequent generation of representatives grow, with many sponsoring others in continuing succession, an organization is created that grows well beyond the efforts of any one individual.

Here's a typical model showing the doubling effect and the power of geometric progression:

You

Sponsor 4 others

Who each sponsor 4 others . . . or 16 representatives

Who each sponsor 4 others . . . or 64 representatives

Who each sponsor 4 others . . . or 256 representatives

Who each sponsor 4 others . . . or 1,024 representatives

And so on . . .

As the original sponsor, you identify your four individuals willing to commit to three core behaviors: *using* your company's products or services, *recommending* them to others, and *sponsoring* other individuals interested in earning an income from these same efforts. You probably won't know many or possibly any of the 256 or 1,024 representatives who show up in your organization on your lower levels. They'll result from your actions of identifying your four business builders who duplicate this prospecting and enrolling behavior.

Of course, no actual organization will look exactly like this or any other growth model. Each organization consists of individuals with various levels of ambition, interpersonal skills, and effectiveness. Some individuals will sponsor many others. Some will sponsor only a few. And many will never sponsor anyone else at all!

This doubling concept can be illustrated by the replication cycle of the simple pond lily. This plant continues to grow and produce a copy of itself on a daily basis. For example, on day 1, there may be 1 lily present on the pond. By day 2, there are 2. Day 3 brings 4 plants. Day 4 shows 8. And so on. Because of the doubling effect, on the day following the one in which half of the pond's surface area is covered by lilies, the entire pond's surface is covered with plants.

This compounding effect also produces another remarkable phenomenon. Initially, utilizing just your own efforts, it will take significant exertion to grow your organization's numbers. This is best accomplished through massive, sustained action. However, as you enroll other business builders, you now have many who are working to duplicate your own efforts. As they continue to enroll others, your group continues to grow geometrically. At some point in the process, the momentum of the doubling effect kicks in. At this point, your organization starts to grow by leaps and bounds. More and more partners flow into your team and more result, in turn, from each of their efforts. Before long, your group is growing without your own personal labors. We discuss in further detail how to generate this rapid momentum in your business.

Since the 1950s, network marketing has survived numerous legal challenges. A set of very specific rules and regulations have been laid down to distinguish the many legitimate, ethical network marketing companies from the illegal pyramid schemes and chain letter deals. These schemes have tarnished the entire industry's reputation and continue to detract from the solid, reputable companies. They confuse the general public about what is legal and legitimate in a customer referral type of business.

In the United States, the Direct Selling Association (DSA) sets the high standards to which ethical network marketing companies subscribe. The DSA has been in existence for more than 100 years, and about 150 of the most proven, ethical, and successful U.S. companies are members who agree to abide by the code of ethics this organization sets forth. These companies comprise about 90 percent of the U.S. sales volume traded by all network marketing companies. The Association's mission is "To protect, serve, and promote the effectiveness of member companies and the independent business people they represent. To ensure that the marketing by member companies of products and/or the direct sales opportunity is conducted with the highest level of business ethics and service to consumers."

Representatives of DSA companies agree to the following high standards:*

- Tell your potential customers who you are, why you're approaching them and what products you are selling.
- Explain how to return a product or cancel an order.

*Reprinted from The Direct Selling Association, www.DSA.org.

- Respect the privacy of your customers by calling at a time that is convenient for them.
- Promptly end a demonstration or presentation at the request of your customer.
- Provide accurate and truthful information regarding the price, quality, quantity, performance, and availability of your product or service.
- Offer a written receipt in language your customers can understand.
- Provide your name and contact information, as well as the contact information of the company you represent.
- Offer a complete description of any warranty or guarantee.

Non-DSA member network marketing companies are estimated to comprise only about 10 percent of all direct sales made in the United States, though they are thought to be about 1,500 in number. Many of these companies are small and poorly funded. As a result, there is often a high failure rate with most of them going out of business within their first three years. Such high turnover has served to give the entire industry a bad reputation. Every time a poorly managed company fails, so do all its distributors along with it. They are forced to painfully watch all their past efforts and the organizations they toiled to build dissolve into oblivion. This epidemic underscores the need to select a well-financed, ethical company with an extraordinary product line and sound business plan. When an independent distributor chooses a stable company to build in, she dramatically improves the odds of her organization enduring into the next century.

Let's look now at the first step in laying a successful foundation upon which a network marketing dynasty can be built—identifying your reasons for joining and crafting a vision to inspire your top achievement.

THE 7 STEP SUCCESS SYSTEM TO BUILDING A $1,000,000 NETWORK MARKETING DYNASTY

Step 1: VISIONING—
ESTABLISH YOUR REASONS FOR JOINING;
CREATE A COMPELLING VISION

Vision is the ability to hear music in the future.
Belief is the ability to dance to it now.

—Jay Davis Clarke

Most people who become involved in network marketing are initially attracted for very specific and personal reasons. Of course, one of the most common reasons involves money—and all of the wonderful things that money provides. For others, motivation may come from a desire to pursue a rewarding, fulfilling, and fun occupation. Others may be attracted to the time and personal freedom that this business can offer. Others still may want to become associated with a supportive team who contribute to the lives of others with either extraordinary products or a potentially life-changing income opportunity. Let's examine several of the different areas of motivation first as they apply to you and then as they relate to creating rich value for your prospects.

BEYOND THE MONEY

Perhaps you were initially attracted to network marketing because you saw it as a way to generate a supplemental

1

income stream. Maybe you had a desire to make life a bit easier for yourself and your family by earning an extra few hundred or a few thousand dollars more each month. Maybe you were attracted to the possibility that this business offered a vehicle to earn at least enough for a new car or home payment. Possibly, your intention was to replace your full-time earned income with a residual income that would free you up to pursue other interests and passions.

No matter what your motivation, it will support you to clarify exactly what you hope to attain from your network marketing efforts. Doing so will both allow you to determine the amount of monthly income that would make your efforts in this business worthwhile and serve as the motivation for doing what oftentimes may be inconvenient or uncomfortable. Your ability to gain clarity regarding what motivates you will be the first step in formulating a detailed plan to achieve the level of income that will make the attainment of your goals and dreams possible. For example, if your goal is to earn a royalty income of $10,000 per month within a few years' time, your action plan will need to be considerably more rigorous than if your goal is to cover a monthly car payment.

Oftentimes, those first introduced to network marketing may know that they want to earn a specific amount of money but will not have sufficient clarity regarding for what purpose they will use the money. It is important not only to know how much income you intend to generate but also why you want the income. Money alone is usually not a sufficient motivator to encourage the sort of consistent and persistent daily action required to build a network marketing dynasty. If you are not clear about why you are doing this business, consider the following possibilities as if money were no object:

- Would you continue to work at your present occupation? Would you retire early or cut back on your work schedule?
- Would you continue to live in your current home and neighborhood? If you'd buy a new house, what would it be like and where would it be located?
- Would you drive a different car and have any new toys?
- How would your family make use of a sizeable recurring income?
- Would you put your children or grandchildren through school?
- Would you pay off all debt and revel in the freedom of being debt-free?
- Would you invest in real estate, stocks, or other investments?
- Would you travel and explore? If so, where?
- Would you go on an extended shopping spree? For what items?
- Would you donate your money or time to a special project or charity?
- Would you pursue any passions or hobbies? Would you take lessons in a craft or sport or develop a new skill?
- Would you develop a secure retirement fund?
- Would you return to school to finish your education or pursue an interest?
- Would you use your network marketing business and the opportunities it provides to take on a personal development program?
- Would you step into leadership in your company, church, or community?

- Would you partner with friends and family to create a fun and rewarding lifestyle?
- Would you free up your time to coach youth sports or do volunteer work?
- Would you use your free time to undertake programs to increase your self-esteem and personal confidence level?

In planning how you will impact your world with your network marketing opportunity, you are limited only by your imagination and creativity. As strange as it may seem, some fear the creation of wealth, thinking it will lead to temptation and corruption. How often have you heard it expressed that money is the root of all evil? Money, in and of itself, is neither good nor evil. It is how we decide to utilize our wealth that determines its character. If you may have feared creating wealth for a similar reason, just ponder how much good you could do to ease some of the world's suffering or how you might provide opportunity for those in need with the wealth you could create using network marketing as your vehicle.

Take a few minutes now and identify what you will be achieving with regard to income and identify your reasons for becoming involved in network marketing. Do not allow yourself to be hindered by self-doubt, a lack of belief or clarity in how you will achieve your desired level of income. I discuss in great detail how to create an action plan that will support your own particular goals and dreams, but before reading on, please answer the following questions:

- If you were to look back upon this day four years from now, how much monthly income would your business need to generate for you to consider your involvement in network marketing one of the best things you have ever done?

- What are your top 10 reasons for becoming involved in network marketing?

1. _____

2. _____

3. _____

4. _____

5. _____

6. _____

7. _____

8. _____

9. _____

10. _____

Create a Compelling Vision

Now that you have identified your top reasons for building a business, it's time to transform these motives into a vibrant, passionate vision that will inspire you and those with whom you'll share your vision. Perhaps your motivation to build a business may start out small. Maybe your reasons are conservative in nature. You may be fairly content with your current work and lifestyle. If this describes your situation, your vision will likely look a lot like an extension of your current lifestyle with some specific improvements in certain areas in which your life is not working optimally. However, if you are among the more ambitious who are seeking to build a network marketing dynasty because of a desire to dramatically impact your life and what's possible by living large, your vision will bear little resemblance to a life marked by the typical daily grind that most others are wrapped up in, with all the suffering, struggle, or lack that limits what most believe is possible to attain. For this vision, I'll assume that your motivation stems from a desire to have it all—a thriving network marketing business that supports your dream lifestyle.

Pretend for a moment that a genie has appeared before you. This genie possesses a magic wand that you can wave over your life, allowing you to transform your current existence into a life of choice. The power of this magic wand can touch every aspect of your life. It can create wealth and abundance in your world for you and for those you love. This abundance will allow you to live in choice, no longer needing to suffer because of a lack of material needs. Your decisions about what you'll have in terms of cars, homes, and other material possessions need no longer be limited because of money.

Moreover, this magic will impact your life well beyond money and material goods. It will influence what you do. Your days will be characterized by a newfound freedom that will allow you to do what you want, when you want to do it. Your typical day at work will take on a whole new empowered energy. You'll be living and working in choice—not because you have to do so. You'll no longer have to answer to the demands of a demeaning boss or deal with difficult employees, peers, or subordinates. Nor will you need to fight rush hour traffic or punch that time clock that used to track the pennies you earned, making someone else wealthy. The stresses of working for someone else will evaporate into the contentment that comes from knowing that your efforts are being truly rewarded. You'll now have the vehicle to earn what you're really worth.

Think for a moment about how you will spend your dramatically increased amount of free time. What will a typical day at play look like for you? You'll be able to do all those things you didn't have the time or money to do before. Will that be a favorite sport or hobby? Maybe it will mean more fun time with family and friends. Remember, the genie has put no limitations on what you can do, so why would you continue to do anything that doesn't honor your values or provide you with fulfillment and happiness?

Think about the legacy you can leave on this planet if you have the time and income to contribute to others. How would you contribute and to whom? Would your generosity extend beyond family to friends in need? Would you adopt a philanthropic mission? What would give you such fulfillment that you could spend the next 100 years contributing to this cause? All this will become part of your vision.

Finally, in addition to all the money, material possessions, and time freedom to do all those great things you've always wanted to pursue, you'll now have the luxury to work *on* yourself. With the need to chase a daily earned income in your past, thanks to the consistent flow of residual income coming into your mailbox each month, you can now focus on the challenge of personal development, if you so desire. You can create a plan to expand who you are, develop those qualities you wish others to know you by, and break through any limitations that have come in the way of achieving happiness and personal fulfillment. Later in this book we speak about personal growth strategies you may want to take on. For now, think about who you will decide to *be* and the qualities you'll embody that others will recognize in you. Will you be known for your charisma and contribution? Will others see you as an inspiration for what's possible to accomplish in life? Will you be known for authenticity and compassion? Perhaps your life will be all about fun, adventure, and the courage to live passionately and without limitations. For what qualities would you like your children and others you respect to know you? These traits will all be part of the reinvented person and lifestyle you'll clarify in your vision.

A vision that inspires you to breakthrough accomplishment must honor your most important values. These values make up the core of who we are.

Which are your most important values?

Love	Security
Fun	Recognition
Happiness	Family
Compassion	Humor
Contribution	Acceptance
Adventure	Appreciation
Beauty	Order
Freedom	Spirituality
Creativity	Harmony
Peace	Safety
Belonging	Joy
Communication	Intimacy

They demand to be honored. If they are violated, you'll likely become angry, withdrawn, and noncommunicative. As you craft your vision, make sure you design all areas of your life in choice. There need not be any *shoulds* that result in pain, struggle, and resentment. As the master architect of your future, you can make everything a reflection of your commitment to live responsibly. Taking responsibility for what manifests itself around you means ensuring all aspects of your life work optimally including the quality of your relationships, your health and physical condition, your wealth and financial security, your happiness, the pursuit of your recreations, hobbies, and passions, and your personal and spiritual development. Who says you can't have it all? It's about time you decided to stop settling for less than you deserve!

Vivid Visions Fuel Self-Motivation

Before you take some time to put your own idealized vision down on paper, let's look a bit deeper at some of the reasons for creating a detailed written vision. Ever cry or scream when watching a movie? We know it's just a movie with actors pretending to step into the roles of their characters. But we cry or become afraid anyway. Now close your eyes. Picture someone running his long pointy fingernails down a black chalkboard. Does this visualization cause a shiver to run down your spine? Perhaps you felt the tingles just by envisioning the scene. The reason for these seemingly illogical responses is that the mind cannot tell the difference between events that are real and those that are vividly imagined. If we can create a vivid mental picture of how our reality will look, sound, smell, and feel, our mind will support us in experiencing it as though it *were* actually real.

Once we create the vivid mental picture of the life we desire, we can then deliberately reinforce these images into our consciousness by daily repetition. By reading our ideal vision daily (once upon rising and once at bedtime is best), it eventually becomes part of our consciousness. The more familiar it becomes, the greater will be our belief in its ultimate realization. Before long, what was once a foreign and difficult concept to grasp will soon become an expectation of what our future will resemble. When such a future appears to be inevitable, we will find ourselves acting in ways that are consistent with its actually happening. The more we can condition our mind to expect such an outcome, the more motivation we will generate to fuel its fulfillment. Do not be limited by thoughts that the vision of your ideal world may be unrealistic and beyond your grasp. The more familiar you become with the concepts presented in your vision statement, the more self-motivated you will become to take the actions necessary to attain your ideals.

The opposite effect holds true as well. If we worry or envision a future that is worse than our current reality, this expectation will result in the creation of self-sabotage. When we see ourselves failing, we create the expectation of failure. Our mind says, "Okay, we're going to fail anyway, so why should we work so hard and do these inconvenient and uncomfortable actions (like prospect friends, family, and strangers) when our efforts are likely to be futile?" We justify behaviors that are inconsistent with success and then get to be right about our expectation of failing after all! Self-sabotage can take many forms. Perhaps it will show up as inconsistency in our prospecting actions, working only when we feel like it. Maybe we will fail to follow up with our prospects because we tell ourselves that they are probably not interested anyway. With an expectation of failure, our conversations will also likely lack the enthusiasm, belief, and value critical in the art of enrollment. We expect to fail and fail we do! Then we make excuses for this outcome, often blaming network marketing itself, our company, our upline support team, or any other convenient victim for our own missing belief and lack of action.

If we see our future as more or less the same as our current situation in life, we will create just enough self-motivation to bring about some successes that will maintain the status quo. Once things start picking up, we'll return to ineffective behaviors consistent with our expectation of more of the same. We'll experience small, incremental changes that are in line with our expectations and actions. The more we experience the same results we have come to expect, the more complacent and apathetic we will become. After all, if things are always likely to stay the same, more or less, why work so hard or become motivated to break through any challenges that may arise? It's no use anyway. We might as well stay safe and secure in the rut we've dug called our comfort zone!

Take a moment now to ask yourself honestly if your current vision for your future is bright and optimistic, negative and depressing, or consistent with what you are currently experiencing. No matter where you now find yourself, you have the ability to craft an empowering and inspirational vision. If we do not deliberately take responsibility for what our lives will be like in every respect, then, by default, we forfeit our ability to choose and create this reality purposefully. If we forgo this right, we must then accept whatever vision others have for our lives. We then lose control over our destiny. Our expectation of having less than we really desire becomes a self-fulfilling prophecy. Like most of the rest of the world's population, we then resign ourselves to a life that neither honors our most important values nor inspires us to be our very best.

It's now time to break this vicious cycle. Your future need not bear a close resemblance to your past. Remember, we *already* have a vision for our futures. For most of us, this is usually just a different version of our past experiences with small, predictable improvements. Just look around you. Do you like what you see? If not, it's now within your power to craft a new and exciting reality to step into. Remember, too, that we will be taking responsibility for manifesting whatever vision we *choose* to manufacture by designing a detailed plan that will answer the question, "What will it take to manifest this vision deliberately in all respects?"

Your vision will inspire you and fuel your motivation to do whatever it takes to result in its being manifested. By sharing it with others, it will also inspire them to join you in its fulfillment, while creating visions of their own. You will be able to tell the quality and strength of your vision by taking a look at the actions it inspires. In network marketing, where you see little activity, you will find a weak and uninspiring vision at its source. As you become adept in crafting your own vivid and compelling vision, you will also be developing the skills necessary to teach others how to create their own empowering visions. Constructing such a vision will always be the first step in building a solid foundation upon which to design the action plan and personal effectiveness structures that will result in the network marketing dynasty you desire.

Not only will your vision fuel your belief level and be the foundation for your action plan, but you will be able to return yourself to your vision whenever the going gets rough and challenges arise, as they are sure to do. Similarly, if your distributors become discouraged and resigned that "this will never work," reminding them of the reasons they became involved in the first place will support them to muster the courage and perseverance needed to hang in there and work toward the realization of their dreams, rather than to quit and forever give up on them.

Writing Your Vision

It's now time to set aside an hour or two and actually put your vision into words. Your written vision will be most powerful when crafted as an already accomplished scene from a movie depicting your life at some point in time. Write your vision in the first person, present tense. "I am now . . . I now have . . . I am doing . . . I am contributing to . . ." and so on. Avoid writing in terms of negative behavior. Instead of writing "I will no longer be poor and overweight," say "I am abundant and healthy." Your mind will key in upon the images created, so craft these images to your advantage. Include in your vision as many sensual references as possible. What are you feeling emotionally? What sights, smells, and sounds are present in the scene you are depicting? What are others who play an important role in your vision saying, doing, and feeling? Make your vision as emotional as possible by focusing upon those areas that will bring you the most joy and fulfillment. Remember to include as many others in your vision as possible, since a vision that is only about you will not inspire or motivate others in the way one that touches their lives will. You'll know that you've hit the mark when you are inspired by reading what you've written.

Following are three examples (Exhibits 1.1 through 1.3) of visions written by successful network marketers to inspire their accomplishments in building their network marketing dynasties.*

Please do not continue to read on until you've written your very own compelling vision. Commit now to reading this vision twice daily, morning and evening—until it is manifested into reality.

*Thanks to Richard Brooke for his groundbreaking work on vision. The concepts offered in this chapter were derived from his Vision Workshop and book *Mach II Starring You!*

Promoting my income opportunity is fun and easy for me. Many people are waiting for me to introduce them to this opportunity. They are ready to go! Everyone I approach is interested. I continue to talk to people every day with enthusiasm and conviction. I ask a lot of questions to find out what things are important to others and what might be missing in their lives. I really listen to others and honor them. People are attracted to me as a result of the kind of person I am. I am courageous. I am a leader. I am having fun. I am enthusiastic. I am extremely organized and on track to attain all of my dreams. My opportunity is a gift. It is the most incredible opportunity on the planet. I am ecstatic about the progress I am making. My group has grown. I am mentoring and training my organization and powerfully developing six leader groups. Their organizations are growing, and they are in love with the journey.

Two powerful couples, Ken and Chris and Ken and Tracy, have stepped into an accelerated leadership role. Each earn at least $5,000 every month. Cindy is earning at least $2,000 monthly, and her life is going so well. They are all excited about the progress they are making. They continue to talk to people every day about the income opportunity with enthusiasm and conviction. All of their visions are manifesting. They expect good things to happen to them. We are all having fun playing full out!

Wow, I'm a member of the president's inner circle! I am so relaxed and at peace. I am earning at least $10,000 every month, like clockwork. It feels good, really good. It has provided us with a very comfortable lifestyle. Tim has totally transitioned out of his practice. We are developing multiple streams of income. Our real estate investments are worth millions!

Exhibit 1.1   Gayle Driscoll's Vision

As a result of our group's progress, our company has grown the most during its twentieth year in business. We have supported each other to achieve our own magnificence. We have all been appointed to the company's advisory board and have contributed our excitement and enthusiasm to the entire distributor force. We have created an incredible law of attraction. Anyone looking for an income opportunity is attracted to our company. Our vision has truly manifested!

I awaken on this glorious day, the sun reflecting off the pristine water on the lake. It's so beautiful to wake up on our own without the blaring sound of an alarm clock. Tim is already sitting on the deck, enjoying the warmth of the early sunshine. I meet him with a glass of freshly squeezed orange juice. We embrace. "Good morning. I love you!" It looks like another joyous day in Coeur d'Alene with not a cloud in the sky. We sit together for several minutes in silence, enjoying our surroundings—especially the calmness of the lake. Tim says to me, "Let's go to breakfast." "Okay," I reply. "Hey, Tim, you know the best thing about going to breakfast today? We don't have to get into a car!"

We both scurry down the dock and jump into our new 29-foot Torpedo wooden boat with bright yellow interior. As we start the boat, Tim looks at me and smiles. I see the spark in his eye. He truly loves where he is in his life.

As we pull away from the dock and make our way to breakfast, I hear our neighbor yell out, "Hey! Congrats on the new house and boat and by the way, the name is absolutely perfect!" V I S I O N is written in large yellow script letters on the back.

"Looks like we made it, babe!" Tim punches the throttle and we scream full out. It's the only sound on the lake! What a grand feeling!

Exhibit 1.1 *(Continued)*

Our Canadian network marketing community is rapidly growing and prospering. New leaders are showing up as I project enthusiasm, confidence, and definiteness of purpose to lead them to success. Our Toronto meetings are exploding in size. The Ottawa group is stepping into leadership and is having their bimonthly regional meetings in the nation's capital. Groups in Barrie, Calgary, Vancouver, and Nova Scotia are also contributing to unprecedented growth in Canada, leading the company in growth and sales. This gives me great satisfaction and peace as the patience, dedication, persistence, and contribution of these pioneering groups is paying off with big returns. Darrin and I have reached the regional leadership level in our company, earning at least $10,000 every month. We have strong, self-sufficient leaders. It is a wonderful, fulfilling feeling to attain this goal in partnership with our leaders, coaches, and mentors. I enjoy every minute of this journey!

We are blessed with an incredible life. Our family is healthy, happy, living in abundance, and enjoying wonderful relationships and friendships. We project a calm and serene energy to others that draws them to us to learn more. We happily and passionately give them access to what is possible and this contribution opens the door for the next success story!

I open my eyes and see that the sun is shining and the sky is a crystal clear blue. A gentle breeze flows through the window as I look out at the lake. I lounge in bed for a little longer, snuggling up to Darrin when the girls come rushing in. They excitedly jump on the bed and clamor for us to get up and get ready for the party. The finishing touches on "Lakefront" were done last week and more than 100 guests are anticipated for our open-house barbeque celebration.

Exhibit 1.2   Khor Balsara's Vision

The momentum and abundance that our network marketing business has provided have taken us to the top; we are flying high with enthusiasm and joy. Today we celebrate with our friends, family, and leaders. We have attracted abundance and prosperity in everything we do. Our lakefront house is simple and elegant, inviting and exuding comfort for all. Outside, the hot tub is steamy and the horizon pool is crystal clear.

We shower, then dress the girls, and tidy their rooms proudly so they can show off their individual decorating creations. They are laughing and working happily together. It is a joyous feeling for me to see them so vibrant and confident in all that they do.

Mom and Dad come over from their bungalow and start fussing over the preparations. They also have a bounce in their step and pride in their faces at our collective accomplishments. They have just advanced to the $5,000 per month leadership level in our company, along with four other leaders in our organization. They have no financial worries and are living their dream retirement of traveling often and enjoying our Canadian summer at "Lakefront."

The first guests have arrived and it does not surprise me that they are Greg, Una, and their family. They come in with a smile and hug all around. Greg says, "Khor, this home is truly magnificent and yet so down to earth. I love it!" I glow with pride and appreciation for Greg for his contribution and love in making this day possible.

More and more arrive. The house is filled with laughter and joy. Children are everywhere running around in delight, playing on the grass, or heading for the pool. Splash! The first child hits the water. Of course, it is my fearless Emma, her long, brown hair streaming after her as she comes out of the water after a perfect dive. Zara,

(Continues)

Exhibit 1.2   *(Continued)*

the natural swimmer, is next. She is followed by Alana, Chrissy, and Sean. Aidan and Justine follow behind with cousin Mehra.

Music is playing and the song "Summer days, oh, summer days, lying in the sun" plays. The barbeque sizzles and smokes, with an abundance of steak, seafood, and grilled vegetables being dished out for everyone to enjoy. The feast of delicious meats, vegetables, and salads is welcome after all the activities of the day. A group just finished beach volleyball and the jet-skiers are riding out on Lake Ontario, just in front of our home. As everyone slows down to eat and chat quietly, I gather their attention and say, "Thank you all for coming to join us to celebrate our new home. It is now complete with your presence! Our family is so blessed to have you all as part of our lives. We love and appreciate you so much."

I feel a tear roll down my cheek as I look into everyone's eyes and see their love. A wave of love and joy overcomes me, and I break out into tears, then laughter. "A special thank-you to our networking partners, who believe in themselves and in us. You are the reason we are here today."

I look around again, meeting everyone's eyes and pouring from my soul happiness, joy, and gratitude. My passion for contribution is being fulfilled while I am true to my values of freedom and fun. "A toast to you all; may you always have health, happiness, and success!"

That night when the kids are in bed, Darrin and I sit alone in the hot tub adjoining the horizon pool. We are sipping our wine and not saying a word. Our energy is one, enjoying the peace, dreamily watching the large, orange sunset over the fragrant and abundant blooms of the rosebushes to the west. Their scent and the fresh lake breeze mingle to create the most serene and surreal end to a wonderful day.

Exhibit 1.2   Khor Balsara's Vision *(Continued)*

As we sit on the beach in Hawaii, we are contemplating our good fortune and the marvelous feeling that comes from living our dreams. Our key leaders have just left after spending a week playing, planning, and enjoying life.

Karen's achievement of the top leadership position in our company prompted the idea for a big celebration in Hawaii. Mary Anne has become a consistent $5,000 per month income earner, and Donna and her group are well on their way to this same level. Pam, our newest six-figure earner, is loving her life in Texas and is busy planning their mountain retreat in Colorado. She has assumed a fabulous leadership role with her organizations in Kansas, Texas, and Colorado and is working in Texas to build an empire. Donna, our daughter, is a stay-at-home mom and has purchased a new SUV. She travels on special, annual family vacations with her network marketing income. Eula is consistently qualifying for leadership level pay and is so pleased with her fabulous organization. Jim and Dorothy are making enough with their network marketing income to allow Jim to retire and enjoy their grandchildren. Our daughter, Shauna, is now making enough money with her network marketing income that it totally supports her mission trips to third-world countries to provide medical care for the needy.

It is wonderful to have leaders who have taken over and are moving their organizations forward with velocity. They have truly taken over the reins of leadership. This has allowed us to sit back and enjoy their success. It is so awesome to see them in front of the room, training for the company and presenting a fabulous new chapter for it.

Our family arrives this afternoon to spend a week with us, playing and enjoying each other's company. Lucky

(Continues)

Exhibit 1.3   Don and Mary Lou Vollmer's Vision

Donna and Shauna get to enjoy both weeks in the fun and sun. We spent one week before everyone arrived and will spend another week after they leave. Four heavenly weeks in paradise! We are discussing having next year's gathering on the Italian Riviera. The time we spend with our family is precious indeed. The grandchildren are growing so fast. Soon they will be leaving home themselves. We have had many enjoyable times with all of them as they have grown up with an extended network marketing family. We spend so much quality time in Chicago with Donna, Doug, Andrew, and Amanda.

The most poignant memories of these past few years are truly seeing our leaders advance and realize their dreams. Their lives have changed so very much, and because of that, they have also changed the lives of many others. So many wonderful projects have evolved as those around us realize their dreams. We also have taken one of our dream trips on the *QEII* on part of our around the world adventure. We still love traveling to exotic lands, always learning to appreciate people of all cultures for their contributions.

We are blessed with good health, which we preserve by working out regularly, maintaining a healthy lifestyle for both body and spirit. We have enjoyed our lifestyle of choice for some time now and can truly say that we are living a life with no regrets. We thank God every day for the abundance that is ours to share with our family, our network marketing family, and others in need. Both of us enjoy taking adult education courses through our local university, gaining knowledge about various cultures and history. Don still enjoys having the latest automobiles and car racing. Mary Lou loves being with her church guitar group. Life is grand!

Exhibit 1.3   Don and Mary Lou Vollmer's Vision *(Continued)*

Step 2: PLANNING—
CREATE A MASTER PLAN THAT WILL SUPPORT YOU TO REALIZE YOUR VISION

If one advances in the direction of his dreams,
one will meet with success unexpected in common hours.
—Henry David Thoreau

Now that you have a vision in place that inspires accomplishment, let's look at what actions are necessary to manifest this vision in the world. Of course, the very heart of any business plan will involve three core behaviors:

1. Use your company's products or services. Always choose your own company's products over those offered by all competitors, and buy from your own business. Become familiar with all your products' applications and the differentiating qualities that make them so special and desirable. Develop an unshakable belief in the value of the income opportunity that your products make possible.

2. Recommend your products or services to others everywhere and on a daily basis. Establish an ever-growing list of retail customers as you identify those who might benefit from your company's products. As you go about your day, listen for opportunities to offer your products to those whom you hear

may have a need for them. In network marketing, retailing your products represents one simple way of introducing others to some of the benefits your company offers. Remember that your company's most exciting product is always your income opportunity. Don't sell your opportunity short by failing to offer it to your customers. Recommend the opportunity by showing your plan and inviting others to join you in business daily. Be proud of your opportunity and offer it without attachment, as you would a most precious gift.

3. Sponsor others into your business who see the value of creating a residual income that can contribute to their lives.

Every strategy and approach that we cover in the remainder of this book is in conjunction with these three core behaviors. Let's now analyze your plan in detail, step by step.

BECOME YOUR OWN BEST CUSTOMER

How can you expect others to buy your products or services if *you* are not a devoted and knowledgeable customer? Replace any competitors' products with your company's offerings. Develop as many product experiences as you can, as you identify your favorite products and what you like so much about them. Speak to others in your company and success line (those who earn commissions from your efforts and those whose efforts generate commissions for you) to learn why each product is unique and special. Learn about all the aggressive uses for each and identify any special groups or target markets that each product or service might appeal to. You'll be targeting these groups specifically in your prospecting efforts and with your sales offerings.

SET UP YOUR OFFICE AND GET READY FOR BUSINESS

As a network marketing professional, you'll want to put into place a number of structures and necessities that will allow you to operate your business smoothly and to make a professional impression on your customers and business prospects. Those already in business for themselves will likely have many of these elements already in place. It is important that those just beginning a home business be aware of how vital these support elements are. These include:

1. Get a good, inexpensive long distance phone plan. If your company offers a plan, subscribe to it immediately. If not, look for a plan that charges less than $.05 per minute. If you plan on speaking long distance for more than 10 hours per month, an unlimited calling plan may be your best bet.

2. Call your local phone company and subscribe to three-way calling. You'll need this feature to connect your prospects with your success line partners who will be making your business presentations for you until you are able to make your own presentations and support *your* team to make theirs. Subscribe to your phone company's voice mail or call-answering plan. You will want to leave your prospects and team members with the most professional impression of your business, and an outdated answering machine just won't do. Record a professional and upbeat message to greet your callers with a warm, inviting communication as their first impression.

3. You'll need a toll-free number to remove any reluctance on the part of your customers or prospects calling you back. You can decide if a toll-free number that ties into your local number and rings in your home office will serve you

best or if a separate toll-free voice mail will be more convenient for you to use. Some toll-free voice mail companies now offer a follow-me service, whereby you can decide if your calls will forward onto your home, office, or cell phone or go directly to voice mail. Some services allow fax transmission to this same number. Others also allow you the convenience of listening to your messages or reading your faxes as e-mail attachments.

4. If you'll be doing business from different locations, a cell phone will come in handy. Select a plan that suits your usage needs, and make sure you include voice mail and three-way calling with your service.

5. Set up a checking account that you'll use exclusively for your network marketing business. Get into the habit of keeping excellent records documenting all your expenses. I suggest using an online checkbook or database software program like Money, Excel, or any other record keeping system that will allow you to enter all your monthly debits and credits in columns marked to identify the nature of your expense. This will facilitate your record keeping and make for easy computations at the end of each month and at the end of each year in preparation for tax time.

6. In this modern era, if your intentions are to build a network marketing dynasty, a computer is a must. Use it to communicate with your customers, prospects, team members, and company via e-mail, write your letters, and organize your information. You'll also need to send and receive faxes. You can set up your computer to do so or buy a fax/copier/scanner to handle all these functions. An online fax service such as efax.com, callwave.com, or jfax.com is also a nice convenience.

7. Professionals need business cards and labels to communicate the right look and impression. If your company of-

fers these items with their logo, order them there. If not, your local office supply store can create some attractive cards and labels. You can also purchase labels to use with your computer or a separate label-maker attachment. You can create very attractive stationery right on your computer as well. If you decide to print your business cards from your computer, make sure you use quality stock and create a professional appearance.

8. If your company offers an automatic shipping program, sign up for it to not only receive your products on a regular monthly basis but to also set the proper example for your team. They will do as you do—not as you say. Auto-ship is also a great way to insure you'll never miss a commission check because you forgot to order products that month.

9. If your company offers a duplicable web site, set yours up. Your web site can be a low cost way to introduce your prospects and display your company's offerings. It also sets another duplicable example for your success team.

10. For those instances when you'll be retailing products or prospecting traditionally (not everyone quite yet is computer literate) order your company's catalogs, prospecting brochures, or audio or videotapes. You'll want to have packages pre-made and on hand at all times so you'll never miss a good prospecting opportunity! Keep a stash readily available in your briefcase, carry bag, car, home, and office.

11. Study all your company's training materials. Learn the value of the compensation plan so you can share its high points enthusiastically. What makes your plan unique and attractive to prospects?

12. Commit to attending all company and success-line sponsored conference calls. If your success-line team or company offers a regularly scheduled opportunity call, commit to listen in and invite at least one guest to three-way call in with

you. If training calls are available, listen in while asking questions and taking notes. Your team will only attend these calls if you do!

13. If your company or success line offers a prerecorded opportunity call, listen in and plan to three-way your prospects. If no such call exists, work with your team to create your own. I discuss how a brief three- or four-minute opportunity call can serve as a great tool to make an overview presentation about your company and products. Such a tool can be used by all, even brand new associates who do not yet know enough to make an intelligent or professional presentation themselves. By having this brief, recorded call in place, your new team members can be empowered to immediately step into prospecting action on their first day. All they need to know how to do is dial a toll-free number!

14. Get the names and phone numbers of all your upline leaders. Your upline are those people who earn commissions as a result of your efforts, so take advantage of their support. Take the initiative by calling each one to introduce yourself so that you can begin to create a powerful partnership with them. Get to know their strengths and areas of expertise. Request their permission to call on them for support in building your business. Create a partnership agreement with your upline leaders, those who will be paid on your efforts. You can also use a similar agreement with each of your downline leaders, those individuals whose efforts will result in your own income growth. See Exhibit 2.1 for a sample of such an agreement.

15. Create your own story letter, introducing others to your company, products, and opportunity. Your story letter will tell how you were introduced and why you decided to become involved with your company to pursue a residual income opportunity. It will need to speak about the quality of

Sponsor's Commitment

As your sponsor, I commit to the following:

1. To train you and mentor you, in partnership with my success line, to achieve whatever level of income you desire.
2. To speak with as many prospects as you can introduce me to, until such time as you are competent to make your own prospecting presentations.
3. To use all the company's products, be on auto-ship, and follow company policies and training suggestions when possible.
4. To stay in action myself, prospecting and setting an example for my team.
5. To make myself available to train, coach, and lead you and your team, always championing you to step into leadership of your own as soon as possible.

New Team Member's Commitment

As your new team member, I commit to the following:

1. To use all the company's products, be on auto-ship, and follow company policies and training suggestions when possible.
2. To make myself available for training, coaching, and other calls so that I can best learn to be effective in building my business.
3. To prospect on a regular, daily basis and to set an example for my own team, until I am earning my desired level of residual income.

Sponsor's signature _____

New team member's signature _____

Exhibit 2.1 Partnership Agreement

the products, the integrity and stability of the company, and the exciting income opportunity available for those who decide to share in the company's profits and growth. See Exhibit 2.2 for an outline of a sample story letter.

16. Organize your daily schedule and track all of your prospecting, follow-up, and training calls on a daily basis. I suggest combining either a PalmPilot or a traditional dayplanner system for use on the road with a desktop or notebook computer at home or at the office. For those who prefer a traditional approach to organization, a great tool is the Powerline System Business Planner, www.powerline systems.ws/planner.html. It was designed specifically to support network marketers in their organizational efforts and serves several functions more efficiently than traditional day-planners.

17. Create your notification names list. The people on this list are those you will want to notify that you are now in business. Some will become your customers. Others will become your business partners. Others will refer you to new customers and business partners. For whatever reason, others will not be interested in becoming either a customer or a business partner. This list consists of anyone and everyone you know or know of. Do not rule anyone out or prejudge that they would not be interested. You will never know who will be and who will not be open to your offer.

Allow me to share a personal experience about prejudging prospects with you. When I first began prospecting, I decided to contact all my former classmates, the majority of whom I had not spoken to in ten years. I prioritized my list with those who I thought would be more interested or better prospects at the top. Being an introvert, I was without great communication skills at the time; this was a daunting

Dear Friend,

   I am writing to share with you an exciting income possibility. I have recently established my own home-based business with the Magnificent Company. I was recently introduced to the Magnificent Company when _____.
(In the next few lines, tell how you were introduced and why you decided to become involved. Also, briefly tell your company's story.) The Magnificent Company is a _____ company that has supported thousands of people just like you and me to build wealth from home. I was first introduced to the Magnificent Company by _____ when _____. I was attracted to _____ and saw how I could create an income that would allow me to _____ (speak your goals and vision for your life).

   I'm writing because I thought of you and respect your business savvy. I would love to explore the possibilities of working with you in partnership to reach your own income goals and the dreams that a significant additional royalty-type income can make possible.

   I'm enclosing a brochure and CD that explain the concept of how our company rewards us to recommend their products and the income opportunity they make possible. I'll call you within the next few days to explain more about this, answer your questions, and explore how this opportunity might contribute to your life. Or feel free to call me at 978-555-5555 at your earliest convenience. I'll look forward to speaking with you soon.

Sincerely,

Your name

Exhibit 2.2   Sample Story Letter

assignment. But I believed in what I was doing and decided to persevere, in spite of my discomfort in making the calls. I called on my top 60 prospects. Many purchased products and became long-term customers. Many were not interested in becoming a customer or building a business. Out of the first 60, four individuals expressed an interest in the income opportunity. All tried briefly and quit. I became discouraged and considered not calling the C names at the bottom of my list. However, my sponsor reminded me of the fact that I was not psychic and couldn't possibly know who my next great leader might be. I accepted his logic and challenge to continue with my calls. The seventy-second person I called was a person I considered to be even quieter and more introverted than I. His name is Bill DiPietro. To my great surprise, he was open to meeting my business partner and me for dinner.

Bill shared that his wife was soon expecting their first child, and they were actually looking for a way to replace her full-time income so that she could stay home with their son. Bill purchased $300 worth of products that night and made an appointment to get started in learning about our business.

What I didn't know was that Bill was an absolute master at creating rapport one on one. Much to my surprise, he became an enrollment machine, signing up leader after new leader. In only a couple of years, Bill built a sizeable six-figure yearly, residual income by creating a growing and dynamic organization for himself and for us, his sponsors.

But the story gets better. One of the first people whom Bill prospected was a good friend and former school roommate. When Bill called to notify his old friend that he had just joined our company, his friend said, "Oh, I joined that company about 18 months ago. I just assumed you would not be interested, so I never called you about it."

That assumption probably cost his friend close to $2 million so far. Of course, when Bill told me, was I thankful his friend had prejudged his interest! So please do not prejudge people. You owe it to them to make their own decisions.

SETTING UP YOUR MASTER PLAN

It's now time for us to speak about the numbers game of network marketing. Speaking with enough people to fill your pipeline with a never-ending stream of interested prospects is critical to achieving success. My sponsor, Dr. Ron Scheele, compared the process to the hobby of coin collecting back in the 1960s when it was fairly common to find rare and valuable silver coins amid one's pocket change. Coin collectors back then knew for a fact that if they sorted through enough coins, they were sure to find some great gems. All it required was sifting through a sufficient quantity of coins to locate the keepers.

Another example that drives home the sorting process required to be successful in network marketing is the process of shucking oysters. If you open a few oysters, you'll likely find only some grains of sand within their shells. However, if you go through enough to insure your success ratios, you're bound to uncover a bunch containing beautiful and valuable pearls. Knowing that the pearls exist in some of the oyster shells should be enough of a powerful motivator to inspire you to keep at the shucking process until the right prize-containing oysters come along.

Sorting for network marketing leaders works the same way. They are *definitely* out there, waiting to be discovered by you. Will you speak with enough to have the odds work in your favor? Or will you quit before your pearls are identified? Just as the numbers can work in your favor, if you do not speak with enough people, you'll be much less likely to identify your leaders.

What's more is that with massive, consistent and persistent action, you will generate the momentum needed to attract your prospects to your opportunity. Speaking with one hundred prospects over the course of a week will produce far greater results than speaking with the same hundred over a year's time. Your energy will be different. You'll have so many people to speak with that you will have no time for neediness or desperation in your voice. If you speak only with a few prospects now and then, you'll be more likely to feel a desperate need to get them in. You won't speak with the confidence and unshakable belief required to communicate the rich value and awesome possibilities that await your prospect. After all, beggars don't make very attractive business partners!

Let's begin our discussion of prospecting by exploring with whom we will be speaking. There will be two basic types of prospects we can consider. The first type represents people we know or encounter in our everyday world. We will have credibility with many of these prospects. With others, we will share any number of traits in common, giving us a starting point to develop rapport by exploring these areas of commonality. The second group represents prospects not currently in our world. These might be introduced to us through various forms of lead generation or by deliberately targeting specific niche markets that are likely to contain prospects who fit our ideal profile, namely the sort of people we are looking for in terms of age, educational background, skills, interests, social and business connections, motivation, and any other traits that we have determined would support success in our business.

A logical place to begin our prospect accumulation activities is with the traditional sources of prospects that network marketers have targeted to build their dynasties for the past 50 years. The number one source of these names will be your names or notification list, as we already touched upon. These represent the people you know or know of whom you will simply *notify* of your new business venture. While informing them of your new venture, take the time to explore their interest in considering a partnership with you or recommending others they know who may be interested in this possibility. And that brings us to Step 3.

Step 3: PROSPECTING—
EFFECTIVE PROSPECTING: WHO, WHERE, HOW, AND HOW MANY?

A prospect is just a business partner you haven't introduced to your opportunity yet.

—Joe Rubino

SHOULD YOU LEAD WITH YOUR PRODUCT OR OPPORTUNITY?

Certain companies have product lines that lend themselves more easily to building with a product-first approach. This technique typically focuses first on establishing an extensive retail customer base. From among the hundreds of satisfied customers you develop, a number of business builders will emerge. The advantage to this approach is that individuals leading with the product will typically generate a cash flow more quickly by creating a customer base. The disadvantage is that this is typically a much slower approach to building significant wealth than leading with the opportunity.

It is my experience that those who prefer to lead with the opportunity usually build deeper, more active organizations resulting in greater long-term residual income. In this approach, retail customers usually come about from the pool of prospects that are *not* interested in the business opportunity.

While both approaches are made possible because of the great value of the products sold, I prefer to specifically target people interested in earning a life-impacting income. These people are usually more motivated to treat their network marketing business seriously and more willing to pursue an aggressive action plan in search of other business builders. On the contrary, those prospects who were first introduced by way of the product will usually adopt this same product approach with others, should they eventually become interested in pursuing the income opportunity as well. This leads to slower growth being duplicated throughout the organizational levels. For the most part, this book details an opportunity approach as the fastest means of building a dynasty.

Let's turn our attention to the many elements that comprise a master prospecting plan of attack. One of the most critical components of designing your plan involves formulating your list of prospects and deciding which pathways are most productive for your prospecting efforts. Let's begin by analyzing how to create your notification list in detail.

Creating Your Notification Names List

To create the most extensive list possible, you'll need to use a few memory joggers. Dig out your address book, holiday card list, business associates, social club, church, and school group lists, and any other names lists you can muster. Think in terms of your friends, neighbors, and relatives and ask yourself, "Whom do *they* know?" List all the merchants and professionals with whom you do business and expand upon your list by thinking of everyone related to each one.

I suggest you create a computerized file of each name. In this file, list name, mailing address, phone, e-mail address, and any other pertinent information you have on each prospect. When I began my business in 1991, before the advent of computers, I wrote my names in a notebook. I've since added names, converting them over to a Microsoft Excel file. I have a column for name, address, phone, e-mail address, and one for all notes I enter following each conversation.

In addition to the names you gather from these lists, take a phone book and start to thumb through the Yellow Pages section by section. Ask yourself, "Whom do I know who is a . . . , or who works in. . . ?"

- Accordion player
- Accountant
- Acrobat
- Actor
- Actuary
- Adjustor
- Adoptee
- Advertising
- Aerial photography
- Ambulance driver
- Aerobics
- Air conditioning
- Air testing
- Airport transportation
- Animals worker
- Animal hospital
- Animal owner
- Animal shelter
- Annuities
- Ant control
- Antique cars
- Antiques dealer
- Anxiety disorders
- Apartment broker
- Appliance sales or repair

- Appraiser
- Aquarium owner
- Architect
- Art gallery
- Artist
- Asbestos removal
- Associations
- Athlete
- Athletic associations
- Attorney
- Auctioneer
- Audiologist
- Auditor
- Auto dealer
- Auto salespeople
- Auto mechanic
- Auto body shop
- Auto detailer
- Auto racer
- Auto renter
- Autograph dealer
- Aviation consultant

And that's only the A's! You can do the same for each other letter of the alphabet. Let your mind explore any and all associations from the different category listings. Rule no one out and have fun expanding your list to several hundred names. Have a friendly contest with others you know to see who can come up with the most names on their lists.

Once you've created your list, you'll be in a great position to start notifying your prospects about your new business while asking them to think about whom they know who may be interested in earning an extra income. Many new to network marketing are hesitant to approach those they know about their income opportunity. This typically stems from a lack of belief in either the network marketing concept or in the networker's confidence that he or she will be successful in building a business while able to support others to do the same. Contact reluctance also usually comes from a concern about bothering friends and relatives who may resent your prospecting efforts. Many new networkers are more concerned with looking good (or not looking bad) and being liked than they are with sharing what could be a life-changing gift. If you are experiencing call reluctance, ask yourself, "With whom would I like to share my success and with whom would I enjoy partnering?" Notice also whether your focus is on yourself (looking good, being liked, and not bothering others) or on contributing your gift to *them*. You won't be timid if you actually concentrate your attention on contributing to another's life without being attached to getting them in!

Also, please remember that your notification list is just one source of prospect names. We discuss many other ways of generating names and expanding our prospect list later in this chapter.

So, How Many Leaders Will You Need to Identify, Champion, and Develop?

The answer to this question depends upon the magnitude of your goals and vision. Your vision will determine the amount of income you'll need to make it happen. The grander your vision, the more money you'll probably need to live life passionately and without limitations. It will support you to *ground* your action plan so that it is in line with the amount of income you'll require to achieve your goals.

To do so, let's begin by defining what a leader is. Though you may hold a different definition, I define a leader as a business builder who conducts his or her business methodically and on a regular, consistent basis. Such an individual would, of course, be a product of the products, most likely on a monthly auto-ship program. He or she would have a names or leads list and speak with prospects on a daily or at least a weekly basis. A leader would follow company policies and procedures, attend most conference calls and company events, and display behavior others would want to aspire to and duplicate.

So, in your company's compensation plan, how many leaders will you need to develop to reach your income targets? Your answer will be somewhat dependent upon whether your compensation plan is a binary plan, unilevel plan, forced matrix plan, or any of the other many variations that compensation plans can take. In any event, let's assume that each of your leaders will develop other leaders themselves, who will also do likewise, and so on down the line. Let's look at a standard geometric model to illustrate this point.

You identify

> 4 leaders, who each identify 4 leaders each or
>
> 16 leaders, who each identify 4 leaders each or
>
> 64 leaders, who each identify 4 leaders each or
>
> 256 leaders, who each identify 4 leaders each or
>
> 1,024 leaders

Adding 4 + 16 + 64 + 256 + 1,024 gives us 1,300 leaders through five levels in your organization. Let's assume that your company necessitates a minimum monthly sales/purchase requirement of $100 per distributor in order to qualify for a monthly commission check. Let's also assume that your company's compensation plan pays out an average of 10 percent per level on the total sales volume generated. Based upon these assumptions, in this model, we would have:

$$1{,}300 \text{ people} \times \$100 \text{ each per month}$$
$$\times \ 10\% \text{ commissions earned on their total volume}$$
$$= \$13{,}000 \text{ per month in residual income earned}$$

So if you were to develop 4 leaders, who developed 4 leaders, who developed 4 leaders, who developed 4 leaders, who developed 4 leaders, you'd earn about $13,000 per month. Of course, no model will resemble exactly what an actual organization will look like. The model will simply serve as a place from which to start to give us an idea regarding how many leaders we will need to develop to earn the amount of income we desire. Therefore, in this example, if we desire to earn $13,000 per month in residual income, we would need to initially focus upon the goal of attracting, training, coaching, and championing at least 4 leaders who agree to take on this same goal, and so forth down through five levels.

If your goal is to earn twice as much residual income monthly, you could either identify and develop 8 leaders, who each identify and develop 4 leaders, or you could support your fifth level leaders to each identify 4 leaders, giving you 4,096 leaders on your sixth level. If your goal is to earn half as much income, you might develop either 2 leaders who each identify and develop 4 leaders, or you might just not need to build your organization as deep. Again, although your company's compensation plan will dictate how many leaders you'll need to identify and develop to reach your desired income level, assuming you'll need at least 4 leaders to create a six-figure yearly income is a safe bet. Just because you've identified your 4 people who fit your description of a leader does not mean it's time to stop prospecting yet! Not only will you likely need to sponsor more than just 4 to identify your greatest business builders, but you'll need to continually inspire your team by demonstrating that you are in massive action by sponsoring many more new distributors on a regular basis throughout your network marketing career.

So How Many Prospecting Conversations Are Enough to Identify Your First 4 Leaders?

The answer to the above question depends upon what your success ratios are. A success ratio is defined as the number of business presentations that are required to enroll one leader into your organization. Every network marketer's success ratios will vary depending upon their credibility with their prospect, enrollment skills, personal effectiveness, and ability to communicate real value. In a later chapter, we speak more about how anyone can further develop such skills deliberately by taking on a personal development plan.

For now, if you've been building your network marketing business for some time and have been tracking the number of presentations you've made and the numbers of leaders that have resulted from this many presentations, you'll have a good idea regarding how many additional presentations you'll need to make to identify additional leaders. However, most people have not taken the time to document these statistics. If that is your situation, I suggest you begin to do so as soon as possible. Simply record each presentation you make (in a prospect management software program like *Act*, notebook, or other permanent record) and highlight the names of the leaders who have resulted from these presentations.

If you are new to the concept of tracking your statistics, but have some enrollment skills and have demonstrated the ability to successfully prospect and enroll others, I suggest you consider the following analogy as representing some general guidelines. In a typical poker deck of cards, there are 52 cards and 4 aces. If you were to shuffle the deck and turn over one card after another, you would reveal a sequence of cards ranging from the low of a 2 to the high of an ace. If you interpret each card flipped over to represent the level of interest and commitment of the prospects with whom you'll be speaking, a 2, 3, 4, or 5 would represent prospects who are really not at all interested in your offer. A 6, 7, 8, or 9 might represent a product customer or one who has a mild interest in exploring the possibility of building a business. A 10, jack, queen, or king might represent a person who has some level of desire to build a network marketing business but has only limited focus or success. Perhaps, they'll enroll some customers or an occasional distributor. An ace would represent someone who is committed to building a business, is open to coaching, and is in a regular, consistent, and persistent level of action. If we assume the numbers that correspond to this analogy, we'd know that if we speak with 52 people, there should be 4 aces who will show up and agree to build a business.

Of course, these numbers are only assumptions. They serve as a starting point to give you a general idea regarding how your prospecting numbers may play out. Perhaps you may find that only one of your 4 aces will go on to build a significant residual income. By speaking with 200 to 500 prospects and tracking your actual statistics, you'll have a much clearer idea regarding how many people you'll need to sort through to find and develop your top business builders.

If you are new to this business and are just beginning to develop your enrollment skills or if you wish to start with a very conservative assumption, I suggest you consider that out of every 100 prospecting conversations, one do-whatever-it takes business builder and leader will emerge who will go on to build a significant organization resulting in the creation of long-term residual income. Along with this one leader, based upon our poker-deck analogy, perhaps seven others per month will build to some lesser level of achievement. Again, remember that this is just an assumption from which to begin tracking our actual numbers. As you actually speak with your next 100 prospects, you'll be recording the results of your conversations in order to take the guesswork out of your statistics. If you set sponsoring goals of two new distributors per week, at least one self-motivated leader with superstar potential should likely result from each month's efforts.

Let's break this assumption down a bit further. Assume that you decide to commit to five quality conversations involving business presentations to your prospects on a daily basis. Let's also assume that you will make these five presentations Monday through Friday, averaging five presentations, five days per week. Since there are approximately four weeks in every month, this plan would result in five presentations made on 20 days each month, totaling 100 presentations per month. If our conservative assumption holds true, you might expect to enroll at least one serious, successful business builder each month. Continue with this plan for six months and you'd likely enroll six such leaders. Again, you'll continually track your success ratios as you work your plan to determine what your exact numbers turn out to be.

One factor that will influence your success ratios will be the time frame in which you conduct your 100 quality conversations. The longer it takes you to have these 100 conversations, the lower your success ratios are likely to be. There is a breakthrough level of expertise and momentum that results from compressing your conversation numbers over a briefer time period.

Another factor that will influence your success ratios will be your diligence in following up your prospects in a timely manner. Many of your leaders will come in on the fourth, seventh, or even the tenth follow-up conversation! The gold really is in the follow-up. Successful follow-up conversations will result in many interested prospects showing up who would have been missed with just casual contact. The diligence with which you conduct your follow-up conversations will show your prospects how serious you are about working your business. For other prospects, the timing of your offering will just not fit into their lives. If you commit to "dripping" on all your prospects on a regular basis, you'll be certain to be there at the right time for some as their life situations change and they become open to exploring your income opportunity.

Make a Regular *Daily Action Commitment.* The best way to ensure considerable numbers of enrollments is to commit to a consistent and persistent plan. Ideal consistency comes when you are in prospecting action daily. If your schedule does not permit you to make a daily action commitment, at least consider making a weekly one.

Depending upon the number of hours you can pledge to devote to your business on a daily or weekly basis, commit to a minimum number of quality conversations, which will involve presenting the income opportunity to your prospects. If your schedule allows, commit to at least one per day. I built my network marketing dynasty from a commitment to make five quality conversations daily for two years. I honored this commitment whether I felt like it—or not. On days when my busy schedule as a full-time practicing dentist did not permit me to make all five calls, I knew that I had these additional presentations to add to my five conversations the next day or two.

Because my commitment was to five quality *income opportunity* conversations, I might have to make 20 calls to get my five presentations in on a particular day. Some networkers instead prefer to commit to a certain number of "dials" daily. This would include answering machine messages and busy signals, as well as successful contacts. Selecting this criteria would necessitate choosing a much higher number of dials in order to reach one's goals. Others might choose a commitment to a certain number of what I'd term *nonquality conversations* (those in which one did not get an opportunity to ask if the prospect might be interested in earning an extra income). Perhaps, a conversation intended to create product sales would fall under this category. These are viable alternatives but not as rigorously demanding as the *quality income opportunity conversation* criteria.

Based upon your assumptions regarding what your success ratios are and the number of leaders you wish to identify in the next 90 days, I invite you to select a daily action commitment that will fit in with the time allowance you are able to devote to your business. If your desire is to build a network marketing dynasty, consider your number accordingly—with one presentation daily (or five presentations weekly) the absolute minimum I'd suggest in aligning with this goal.

Please note that I have focused upon how to identify and build leaders, not sales volume. Your organizational volume will naturally grow as you identify and champion leaders to achieve their own levels of success. It will be much more productive to direct your efforts on supporting people to succeed rather than simply chasing volume. Of course, as your leaders use your company's products, recommend, and retail their favorites to others, and sponsor others interested in earning an income, sales volume will naturally flow through your organization.

Let's now turn our attention to some other key components of successful prospecting.

Local versus Long-Distance Prospecting

In this technological age, complete with computers, e-mail, chat rooms, faxes, teleconference bridges, cellular phones, voice mail, jet travel, and a variety of other support structures to aid in communication, your prospecting efforts can focus across your neighbor's fence or all the way across the country or the globe almost as easily. No matter how or where you obtain your prospect's name, you will still need to build an effective, nurturing, and supportive relationship that allows you to best communicate with and champion your new business partner's success. Because it is simpler and at times easier to provide this support with face-to-face local meetings, I suggest you might begin your prospecting endeavors in your home state or local community, if possible. All things being equal, why not launch your prospecting actions close to home? By being able to meet regularly with your prospects and eventual team members, you'll more easily be in a position to build relationships and strengthen your partnerships if you are close by. As you run out of local leads or decide to adopt long distance lead generation methods, you can always expand to neighboring states and regions before targeting more distant prospecting sources.

However, many prospecting methodologies may require a long distance approach. Perhaps, you'll advertise in national publications, purchase opportunity-seeker lead lists containing names of prospects located anywhere in the world, or gather leads on the Internet. Remember, it is your responsibility as your new team member's sponsor and business partner to effectively train her, speak with her prospects, and support her business building success, no matter how far away you live from each other. It will be easier to build such long distance organizations if local and regional meetings exist throughout the countries in which your company does business. Establish partnerships with leaders in other areas, and agree to support each other's local distributors by welcoming them to meetings and working effectively to train cross-line. I later discuss how to put into place effective training and support structures for both local and long distance sponsoring.

DESIGNING YOUR PROSPECTING PLAN IN DETAIL

A successful prospecting plan can be as varied as the number of distributors in any company. Each person will possess different interests, strengths, and focuses. Because of this, different people will find different ways of achieving success. Earlier in this book, I discussed a traditional warm market approach, which would involve contacting the prospects on a notification list. This is a great approach for those who are willing to speak with those they know personally or those they know of. I suggest it as a great place to begin one's network marketing business for a number of reasons. First, the people on this list typically include those who know, trust, and love us. They are often people with whom we have credibility. Many on this list will want to support our success and many will be honored and moved by the fact that we decided to offer a business partnership to them. Oftentimes, it will be the people on our notification list with whom we would most enjoy working and derive the greatest amount of satisfaction from their success. After all, if we really believe in what we are doing and are confident of our impending success, why wouldn't we want to include our friends, family, and acquaintances in our good fortune? Moreover, we already have these names and their contact information. It will cost us nothing in terms of lead generation expenses to start our prospecting efforts with this group.

To the contrary, many beginning networkers feel awkward or reluctant to contact the people they know best. Maybe this is because those who know them well are so familiar with their faults and personal struggles that they lack credibility for them as potential business partners. Perhaps, it is because they do not wish to have these people feel obligated in any way to buy products or join their business as a favor to them. Their reluctance might stem from their own personal doubts about whether they can become successful and whether they can transfer this success to those they know. If this reason is at the source of your reluctance to contact your own notification names list, I suggest you speak with other successful leaders in your company and re-establish your belief in what you are doing and in your eventual ability to succeed in your business building efforts.

In addition to a warm market list, there are many other sources of prospects one might focus upon to fuel business growth. Let's look at what some of the more productive sources of prospect names might be.

Cold Calling Approaches—In Person and By Phone

A cold calling approach is typically not well-suited for the faint of heart. Because you would have no prior relationship established with these cold prospects, you will need to become expert at rapidly developing rapport with your prospect while immediately creating value. It is often a good idea to internalize a basic opening line or script so that you can become adept at sparking your prospect's interest and arousing their curiosity to want to learn more about your offering.

A cold calling approach is particularly well-suited for contacting business owners who may have a need for your products or services. These same prospects may also have an interest in recommending your company's products or income opportunity to their sphere of influence, their customers and fellow business owners. Cold calling can be done in person, in a manner resembling traditional door-to-door sales or it can be done entirely over the phone. It also might involve scheduling a follow-up meeting in person, if your interested prospect is situated locally to you. Taking a phone approach will allow you to be much more productive in going through the numbers to identify those who are interested in learning more. However, with some products that require a demonstration, you may experience much more effective results from actually calling on your prospects in person. I suggest you test both ways, track your success ratios, and continue to follow whichever plan proves to be more productive.

Productive cold calls target business prospects whose customers may have a need for your products or services. When approaching business owners, it is best to be able to clearly and powerfully outline the reason for your call or contact while spelling out the benefits your company offers that may appeal to the decision maker. Some of these benefits include products to support a customer's health, appearance, or other needs or services that save customers money or enhance the user's lifestyle. Additional benefits that may interest the business owner might be the ability to create a second profit center or offer a value-added service to increase customer or client satisfaction. Adding superior products might offer a reason for customers to return more often to the establishment to purchase products and thus help the business to grow.

Another benefit that might be offered could be to invite the business owner and employees to share in your company's profits by spreading the word. Many will want to recommend products or services that they love to others anyway, so why not allow them to get paid for doing so?

Many businesses also lend themselves to easily prospecting their customers or clients in a very professional manner. Attractive catalogs and brochures can be handed to customers or sent to them by mail. Postcards, bill stuffers, or direct mail letters can also be mailed, notifying clients with whom the business already has credibility of the value of additional products or services.

Other businesses may choose to show professional, company-produced video or DVD presentations to expose their clients to the possibilities offered by your company's products and income opportunity. Some may wish to place an attractive sign inviting customers to inquire about your opportunity. Many salons, barbers, realtors, flea markets, gyms, stores, cleaners, tanning salons, and a myriad of other businesses might place a sign that says:

Earn an Extra $2,000/month,

Ask Us for a FREE Brochure and Video.

Like other methods of prospecting, cold calling comes down to a numbers game. If you are convinced that the prospects you decide to target would benefit from your products or opportunity AND you become adept at creating value so that they can appreciate your presentations, success will result. If you choose to take this approach, track your ratios (the number of businesses you'll need to prospect to make a sale or enroll as a distributor) and speak with enough people to make the numbers work.

Remember to always be truthful with your prospect with regard to the reason for your contact, request a brief amount of their time to share the benefits (initially no more than five minutes) and never argue or exert pressure upon them to buy or evaluate your opportunity.

Karen Guzzo of Denver, Colorado, is a master of the art of cold calling. She targets niche-specific businesses that sell to customers or clients who need her company's products. Her energy is bubbly and upbeat but always courteous and nonintrusive as she calls upon her lists of hundreds of businesses that fit the profile she has determined to need her company's offerings. Karen alternates her efforts between phone calling to set appointments and dropping in on businesses that fit her target market. To Karen, rejection means only that she is closer to a yes. Her statistics have proven that if she approaches enough of these niche-related businesses, she will come away with enough interested parties to make her efforts worthwhile. By using this approach, it is not uncommon for Karen to enroll five new distributors weekly with clients who will purchase hundreds of dollars of her company's products each month.

The Three-Foot Rule

While cold calling typically refers to approaching business owners, the Three-Foot Rule pertains to everyone else. This approach assumes that we meet prospects who would have an interest in joining our business every day of our lives. They can be found at the supermarket, PTA meeting, soccer game, and every other place we go. We just never can tell when we might bump into our next superstar business builder. People need what our company has to offer. Furthermore, we can never prejudge who might be interested, if we do not ask. The Three-Foot Rule assumes that it is our responsibility to build rapport and create an opening to explore interest in our offering everywhere we go.

Those distributors who are most successful in building their businesses in this manner share a number of common characteristics:

- They are not afraid to speak with strangers. A stranger is only a friend they have not yet met.
- They are masters at breaking the ice. They instantly build rapport by talking about whatever seems to come up at that particular time and place. They are adept at asking questions to determine if the suspect is really a prospect in disguise.
- They usually have practiced a fluid method of creating an opening with their prospects to take a look. Their pitch comes across in a natural and appropriate manner. Their conversations cannot appear canned, filled with clichés, or pushy and invasive. They must flow naturally as they make a friend while presenting their invitation to explore possibilities without being offensive.
- They are always prepared with business cards, prospecting packages, audio or videotapes, and any other materials used to educate and expose their prospects to their company's products and opportunity.
- They ask questions that stimulate conversation. For example, they might say something like, "I think I've seen you here at these games before. Do you live or work in this area? Oh, great. Can I ask you what you do for a living?"

The areas critical to building rapport are typically: family, where they live, what they do for an occupation, and what their passions or hobbies are. I remember these areas as *FLOP*, since it's critical to develop rapport in order to avoid making your conversation a flop!

- They are adept at making requests that move their prospect along in the evaluation process. They might say something like, "You know you have a great personality and I'm looking for someone just like you to expand my business here in Massachusetts. The position I'm looking to fill has the potential to be VERY lucrative for the right person. Would you be willing to *just* take a look at some information and watch a brief video that describes how our company works? Great! I have an info pack in my car. It's parked right in front. Here's my business card. Do you have one also? Do you think you'd be able to watch this video by Wednesday evening? Would it be convenient for me to call you this Thursday or Friday to answer any questions you may have and further explore your interest? Great! Which night, Thursday or Friday and what time range works best for you? I'll look forward to calling you then! Have a great day."

- Many networkers have successfully built their dynasties by committing to the daily action of handing out a minimum number of audiotapes, CD or DVD ROM presentations every single day. Of course, developing rapport before making the request to evaluate the tool and obtaining a commitment to watch or listen to the presentation, and agree to speak about their interest on follow-up will dramatically increase the effectiveness of this sort of activity. I suggest always requesting the prospect's contact information before passing out costly materials.

Advertising for Prospects

Advertising can take many different forms ranging from print media (newspapers, magazines, newsletters, bulletins, flyers, billboards, posters, and mailers) to radio, television, and of course, the Internet. Print ads can also vary from the inexpensive small town weekly classified ad to the four-color full-page ad in a major national magazine or newspaper, costing $50,000 or more.

The most effective ads create rich value-laden benefits for their readers. The more effective they are at specifically targeting their intended customers or prospects with those benefits most important to them, the more responses they will draw and the more qualified those leads will be. Both classified and display ads have proven effective at times in targeting prospective network marketers or selling products to interested end users. Classified ads can range from a low of about $10 for a small ad in a weekly town paper to several hundred dollars or more when placed in a large-circulation magazine or journal.

The most effective classified ads specifically call their intended prospects by name. They do this by identifying those benefits most important to the type of prospect they seek to attract. Successful classified ads can target general work-at-home income seekers, entrepreneurial opportunity seekers, or they can hone in on specific niches or occupations to further qualify the respondents by category. Different ads work better in different places and at different times of the year. A work-at-home ad typically draws better in a small-town, weekly newspaper as opposed to the classified section of a major city's newspaper where a more professional prospect might apply. I have had great success with classifieds that target specific professions or groups. I place these ads in various industry-specific journals, magazines, and newsletters. They pre-qualify the prospect by inviting the niche-related applicants to respond. This strategy works particularly well when there is a link between a company's products and a group who may have a use for them. For example, if your company markets a hand cleaner, you might target mechanics, painters, laborers, or any other group that would likely use this product. You might advertise in magazines, newspapers, newsletters, or with flyers targeting the group you are intending to attract. If you're marketing a service like an insurance product, you might target insurance agents, professional salespeople, or those with a particular need for the service.

One important consideration that applies to all advertising is if you advertise product, you'll attract mainly product users. If your desire is to attract business builders, you'll want to advertise your company's most exciting product—your income opportunity!

The following are a number of classified ads that have worked particularly well for our organization. You'll want to alter any ad you select to apply to your own company's strengths and target markets.

Traditional Classified Ads

Partner with Doctors—Earn a Doctor's Income. Health professional network company seeks self-starters to work with dentists, MDs and veterinarians. Call 800-999-9999.

(Help Wanted) Medical professionals, nurses, techs—work from home in partnership with doctors. Your own business with dream income potential. Free info package. Call 800-999-9999.

Stay in Your Pajamas! Pick up a second income without having to get a 2nd job! Pleasant. Respectable. Free details. Call 800-999-9999.

Wake up to Dream Income in 90 days! Process patented weight-loss orders from your location. Pleasant, respectable. Call 800-999-9999.

Rapid weight loss—9 pounds in 9 weeks. Guaranteed 100% safe. Plus, pick up a second income without getting a second job. Free Sample and Video Tape. Call 800-999-9999.

Get paid to lose weight—100% safe. Guaranteed effective! Great for stay-at-home moms! Call 800-999-9999.

A Dream Income Potential—Doctors' professional network seeks partners to join our elite marketing team. For free audiotape, call 800-999-9999.

Teachers, Coaches, and Trainers wanted: Earn an exciting income from home by teaching others our proven turnkey system. For interview, call 800-999-9999.

International Company expanding into NY Health Care Market: Nurses, MDs and other Health Care Professionals Wanted for Non-Clinical Opportunity. Call 800-999-9999.

Tanning salons, Massage Therapists, and Hair Salon Owners Wanted. Earn a Second Income Without Getting a Second Job. Free Video Tells All. Call 800-999-9999.

Earn $2,000 weekly with 8 Easy Sales of high demand breakthrough environmental product. Full training and support provided. Call 800-999-9999.

"Millionaire Makers"—That's what *Success Magazine* called us in their cover story because of our ability to help you be financially free. To learn how we can help you realize YOUR dreams, call 800-999-9999.

Fun, Money, Travel . . . Enthusiastic self-starters wanted for lucrative income opportunity. Free info pack.
Call 800-999-9999.

Business professionals wanted to follow proven wealth-building system. 4-Year Retirement Plan. Call 800-999-9999.

Are you earning $10,000/month? Call 800-999-9999 to let us show you EXACTLY how you can earn that and more with us.

Attention: Experienced network marketers wanted for lucrative partnership. Company growth means wealth from following our proven plan. Call 800-999-9999 for FREE Video.

Teach & Grow Rich! Public Speakers Wanted—Top leaders now earning FT incomes PT. For Interview, call 800-999-9999 M–F.

Stay home! Partner with Doctors for Full-Time Income with Part-Time Effort. Full training and support. Free details. Call 800-999-9999.

Earn a Full-Time Income with a Part-Time Effort. Complete Training and Support. For your FREE CD ROM and Info Pack, call 800-999-9999 or e-mail WorkAtHome@grand.com.

Teachers wanted to teach others how to become financially independent. Full training provided. Earn what you're worth with us! Call 800-999-9999.

Help others save money on their utility bills and get paid to do it! FT income potential working from your home. Call 800-999-9999.

"We Create Millionaires"—That's what *Success Magazine* said about Drs. Joe Rubino and Tom Ventullo in its December '95 cover story. If you are interested in earning a very substantial income and would like to explore the possibility of partnering with two of America's leading doctors whom *Success* calls the "Entrepreneurial Elite," call us at (800) 999-9999.

WHAT IF: YOU COULD RETIRE IN 2 TO 4 YEARS WITHOUT A PAY CUT? OR YOU COULD EARN A SUBSTANTIAL SECOND INCOME ALLOWING YOU TO WORK ONLY IF YOU CHOOSE TO?
    At age 37, we retired from dentistry with a high 5-figure monthly income that allows us to now support other professionals in achieving the same financial freedom we enjoy. If you are interested enough to have a conversation to explore the possibilities of what our network can provide you, call (800) 999-9999 today. You have everything to gain.

Doctor: Would you be interested in a safe, scientifically proven, affordable way to improve your patients' nutritional status? Are you looking for a second profit center? We have a Professional Support Program to support both options. No billing, no inventory to buy, no shipping or handling costs, with monthly paid retail profits. For FREE details, call 800-999-9999 today!

Where to Place Classified Ads

For a listing of newspapers in the United States and world-wide, visit www.refdesk.com/paper.html.

For a listing of Statewide Press Associations where you can place classified ads, visit www.webdms.com/~ina/assn .html.

Internet Classified Ads

- Work at Home on Your Computer. Fully automated on-line business
- FREE test-drive guarantees success in 30 days
- Pleasant, respectable
- BE PROFITABLE day 1 and get PAID over & over, every week!

Visit www.magnificentcompany.com and let us PROVE how easy earning money at home can be!

If you can send e-mails, you can make money with our fully automated online system.

- FREE 30-day test drive will prove you can be successful in building wealth.
- You make money without the struggle of other home businesses just by following our simple turnkey online system.
- You can be profitable your first day!
- And you get paid over and over, every week once you set the wealth builder in motion!
- We show you EXACTLY how to make money with full support and training!
- Our 20-year-old company enjoys the finest reputation for supporting people to work at home.
- Visit www.magnificentcompany.com and let us prove how easy earning money at home can be!

Earn an income from home working on your computer! We'll prove how simple it is . . . if you can send e-mails, you can make money. Visit www.magnificentcompany.com and take a FREE test-drive tour. Our fully automated system will make you money!

A Word of Warning about Internet Ads.   Regarding Internet classified ads, there are many web sites and online newsletters that offer classified advertising. Be aware that advertising on the Internet is like advertising in the Wild West! I suggest avoiding "free-for-all" sites and the many sites that offer you a free ad in return for some gimmick like viewing other free classified ads. These sites are typically a haven for spammers and scam artists. By associating with them, you will both diminish your company's credibility and set yourself up for a barrage of return spam. You also will waste a lot of precious time that could have been spent on proven ways to build your network marketing business. If you feel the need to try such sites, go to www.hotmail.com or www.yahoo.com first and get a free "disposable" e-mail address that you can just walk away from if and when you become inundated with offers from every spammer on the Net.

I have found that the most reliable place to advertise using classified ads on the Internet is in the paid classified advertising sections offered by many well-respected, niche-targeted newsletters that reach tens or hundreds of thousands of subscribers who have opted in to request the receipt of that particular newsletter.

Here are some sites to place a classified ad online or otherwise get the word out by means of the Internet. I do not endorse any nor can I guarantee the integrity of any of these sites. In fact, because Internet classified ad and prospecting support sites come and go so quickly, some may no longer be viable possibilities by the time you read this. Remember, you may want to get a disposable e-mail address to use for your on-line advertising efforts. That said—here's a list for you to check out:

http://www.classifiedconnection.com/
http://www.ad-to-the-web.com/
http://www.inetgiant.com/
http://www.101-website-traffic.com/?hop=mikefwt.75
   million
http://www.ablewise.com/
http://www.123link.com/
http://www.1second.com/1america.htm
http://boards1.ivillage.com/messages/get/wfhomeopps
   1231.html
http://www.refdesk.com/free.html
http://www.freeclassifieds.com/FreeAds/FreeClassifieds
   .htm
http://www.money-at-home.com/classifieds.html
http://www.iwr.com/free/classads1.htm
http://www.worldwidephotoads.com/cgi-bin/waw
   /viewads.pl
http://www.ecki.com/links/
http://www.business8.com/freead/
http://masterbanners.com/index.shtml
http://www.ad-line.com/
http://www.freeclassifiedads.com/
http://www.thmg.com/free/
http://www.boconline.com/
http://ep.com/js/csp/36745.html

Here are some links to place classified ads and generate additional leads online:

http://www.meer.net/~johnl/e-zine-list/zines/
http://www.ezineuniversity.com/
http://ezine-universe.com/
http://www.worldabooks.com/search-it/ezine/
http://emailingads.com/
http://www.ezineadauction.com/
http://411iservices.com/
http://www.targetmails.com/emails.htm
http://www.emailists.com/category.htm?&session_file=un
defined
http://www.permissiondirect.com/coregistration/index
.html
http://www.flyingpost.com/index.html
http://www.cooleremail.com/services.shtml

And still some further sites that offer lead generation services and other tools:

http://www.emailresults.com/
http://www.glocksoft.com/amlv/
http://successpub.com/
http://www.safelistsoftware.com/
http://www.infacta.com/
http://www.pivotal.com/
http://adturn.com/
https://www.goclick.com/acct/register.mod

Display Ads

Display ads can be a very effective, though costly, means of advertising for business builders. Typically, such ads can run anywhere from $500 to $50,000 or more per insertion, depending upon the publication's circulation and prestige factor.

Running these ads is only feasible when their cost and risk are shared by a number of distributors. Running a co-operative advertising campaign means offering an advertising share for a fraction of the cost necessary to design and place the ad. For example, if the cost of a display ad is $4,000, 16 equal ad slots each costing $250 might be offered to the members of a success-line or cross-line to the members of the entire company. Such a campaign is usually coordinated by an organizational leader who then redirects all leads generated on a round-robin basis to each member taking part in the campaign. Display ads can have interested readers call a toll-free number or respond to an e-mail address. It is easiest to redistribute such responses if a voice mail system is used. The leads can be automatically redirected to the campaign coordinator's e-mail inbox as an audiofile. He or she can then simply forward the lead to the e-mail address of the co-op participant who is in line to receive the next lead. One such voice mail service offering this feature is the Communikate system offered by www.Webley.com.

Successful display ads share a number of the following common characteristics:

- They target the readership of the publication in which they appear. An ad containing benefits that attorneys would be interested in receiving might appear in a law journal or magazine. If your product line may be attractive to plumbers, these benefits would need to be highlighted in an ad appearing in a plumbers' publication. You can see why an ad focused on benefits to attorneys would fail miserably in a plumbers' magazine.
- They are benefit driven and supported by features. Benefits are about your prospect. Features are about you or your company. You'll want to list the most compelling

benefits that your target audience would be attracted to
and then back these benefits up with solid features that reinforce your credibility.

- They should feature an attractive or eye-catching graphic
  or photo that demands attention and causes readers to
  want to read further.

- They can include powerful testimonials that lend credibility to your company, products, and income opportunity.

- Remember that ads that focus too strongly on products
  may not generate enough sales to pay for their cost. It will
  support you to determine what the amount of profit is for
  each sale and calculate the number of sales needed to
  break even with any product-driven ad.

- Ads that focus on your income opportunity have a better
  probability to be cost-effective. Determine what the value
  of attracting a business builder is and calculate the number of business builders an ad would need to draw to be
  cost-effective.

- Consider testing a smaller display ad that is still large
  enough to attract attention. Sometimes a half- or third-
  page ad strategically placed can stand out and generate
  more cost-effective leads than a larger one. Dramatic two-
  color ads can sometimes be as or more cost-effective than
  four-color ads.

- Repetition of an ad in subsequent issues of a publication
  can increase the credibility of a company that continues to
  maintain an ad presence. Though it may attract new readers and additional prospects who eventually realize the
  value presented, it is usually financially unwise to continue to run an ad that did not pull adequately the first
  time it was placed.

- Look for publications that offer reader-response cards that
  invite readers to circle a number corresponding to any ads

that they find interesting. Such a service will increase the number of responses generated while lowering the eventual cost-per-lead ratio.

- Offer a free report, information package, or other perk to encourage readers to respond. Place a call to action after the phone number to increase reader response.
- Research remnant ad space to lower your advertising costs. Some publications offer a substantial discount in exchange for your flexibility in awaiting an issue where the publication has extra, unsold space that is offered at dramatically lower prices.

Note: To maintain impartiality, all the sample advertisements in Figures 3.1 to 3.9 feature the fictional Magnificent and ABC companies.

More on Deciding Where to Place Your Print Advertisements

All advertising will be more effective in soliciting replies from your ideal prospects if you specifically target the types of prospects you desire by inviting them as a group to respond, offering value that appeals to your targeted group, and advertising in niche publications that are read by this crowd. Include the occupations of your ideal prospects in your headlines to attract them while discouraging nonqualified applicants from responding to your ad. For example, to sell an insurance product to the professionals you wish to target, specify "Wanted: Insurance Agents, Attorneys, and Accountants for Lucrative Part-Time Opportunity. International NYSE Company Expands into California Market." To the extent that you can zoom in and target a particular type of prospect, you will attract a qualified individual who will better relate to your opportunity.

Join 10,000 Leading Health Care Professionals in Recommending the Finest Pet Care Products Available

Magnificent Pet Care
Pet Dental Solution
Pet Gel
Pet Toothbrush
Pet Ear Cleaner
Pet Shampoo
Pet Deodorizer
Pet Antioxidant
Pet Relaxant
Air Purification

- Safe, Effective Products That Support Pet Health and Wellness

- No-Risk Clinical Trials

- $50 – $100 in FREE Product with Trial Programs

- Add an Additional $25,000 to Your Practice's Bottom Line This Year

- Lucrative Staff Bonus Programs Give Staff a $200 Weekly Raise at No Cost to the Practice

- For FREE details, visit www.magnificentcompany.com

- or e-mail: Magnificent@abcco.com

Figure 3.1 The Magnificent Company Pet Care

Radio Ads

Radio offers yet another cost-effective medium for effective network marketing ads. Successful radio ads, like all other forms of advertisements, are benefit driven and target the exact profile of the customers or prospects you wish to attract. They usually focus on one predominant benefit that causes readers to perk up and pay attention. Because many listeners will be hearing your radio ads while they are in their cars, it is important to have an

---

Where Will *You* Be Financially in 4 Years?

In the past four years, Dennis Pezi has built an income that's given him quality FREE TIME to spend with his family.

Learn How You Can

- Create New Income Streams that can add $2,000 to $8,000 Monthly to your bottom line
- Enhance the Image of your Business with Cutting Edge Services
- Reduce your Tax Liability
- Develop a Royalty Income that can Supplement or Surpass Your Current Income and Provide You With Quality Free Time

Just four short years ago, Dennis Pezi was working 50 hours a week and getting nowhere fast. His wife, Bonnie, was working 40 hours a week as an office manager. That's when he was introduced to The Magnificent Company by his school classmate. Immediately he saw a way for him and his family to exit the rat race and have more time to enjoy life. Today, Dennis is dedicated to supporting others to enjoy this same freedom of choice in their lives. If more free time and financial security interests you, call today for more details: 800-999-9999.

Figure 3.2 Where Will You Be Financially in 4 Years?

easy to remember toll-free phone number that listeners can recall and dial. (See Exhibits 3.1 and 3.2 on pages 76 and 77.)

Radio effectiveness as an advertising medium and audiences differ significantly by station, strength of signal, population density, and time of day. Be sure to select a station whose listeners fit the profile of your perfect prospect. If you're seeking 30- to 50-year-old professionally oriented prospects, you wouldn't want to advertise on rap or hip hop music stations. Numbers of

Figure 3.3   Niche Market Display Ad

LEARN HOW TO:
- Add lucrative auxiliary-driven profit centers.
- Attract new patients with the latest techniques.
- Increase practice income without working harder.
- Enhance your image with value-added care.
- Practice because you choose to, not because you have to.
- Add an extra $2,000 to $5,000 per month to your practice's Bottom Line.

With the programs you'll read about in:

Opportunities in Dentistry Magazine

FOR YOUR FREE COPY, CALL 800-999-9999 or E-mail: DrJRubino@Email.com.

Figure 3.4 Add an Extra $2,000 to $5,000 per Month to Your Practice's Bottom Line

listeners also increase dramatically during morning and afternoon drive times with the fewest numbers of listeners present in the overnight time slots. Many radio stations offer a "run of the station" package in which they agree to air your ads during time slots that they select. Beware that this often means running your ads in the early morning hours when few listeners will hear your offer. Like other forms of advertising, it is prudent to conduct a limited test of each ad you wish to run before committing to a widespread campaign.

For a listing of radio stations in your area, visit

http://www.radio-locator.com/cgi-bin/home or
http://windowsmedia.com/radiotuner/MyRadio.asp.

With The Prosperous Dentist Financial Growth System, many dentists have added $3,000 – $8,000 to their monthly income.

Will YOU be next?

Learn How You Can . . .

- Increase Practice Profitability
- Provide Cutting Edge Services To Your Patients
- Create New Profit Centers That Can Add $2,000 To $8,000 Or More Monthly To Your Bottom Line
- Enhance The Image Of Your Practice
- Implement Significant Tax Reduction Strategies
- Develop A Royalty Income That Can Supplement Or Even Surpass Your Professional Income
- Create Quality Free Time To Enjoy Your Wealth

For More Information, Call:

800-999-9999

The Prosperous Dentist

Financial Growth System

. . . committed to your success

Figure 3.5   Dental Niche Ad

Television Ads or Info-Commercials

Several network marketing companies have pioneered very successful television ads and infomercials. Due to the exorbitant cost to coordinate, produce, and air a professional-looking ad or info-commercial, such projects are typically reserved for network marketing companies themselves or large organizations with the support of their parent company. With TV advertisements, it is critically important that a professional production company be used that is knowledgeable about this advertising format. Qualified production companies have a

Only 4% of Dentists Will Retire Financially Free.
Will YOU Be One Of Them?

Learn How You Can . . .
- Increase Practice Profitability
- Provide Cutting Edge Services To Your Patients
- Create New Profit Centers That Can Add $2,000 To $8,000 Or More Monthly To Your Bottom Line
- Enhance The Image Of Your Practice
- Implement Significant Tax Reduction Strategies
- Develop A Royalty Income That Can Supplement Or Even Surpass Your Professional Income
- Create Quality Free Time To Enjoy Your Wealth

Just two years ago, Dr. Tim Driscoll was looking for a way to support his patients to be healthier, while increasing his practice profitability. Not only did he add an extra $3,000 per month to his practice income through *The Prosperous Dentist – ABC Co. Profit Centers*, but he was able to develop a royalty income with a part time effort that allows him to practice in choice and his wife Gayle to stay home full time with their children. Today, Tim is committed to supporting other dentists to increase their incomes, and to spend more quality time with their families and practice because they *choose to* not because they have to. If financial security and time freedom interest you, call today.

Dr. Tim Driscoll, wife Gayle, & Children

Call
800-999-9999

For More Information

The
Prosperous Dentist
Financial Growth System
. . . committed to your success

Figure 3.6 Dental Journal Ad

history of producing successful ads or info-commercials for other companies. The resultant commercial produced must be made without therapeutic or income claims. Failure to pay significant attention to these and other Federal Trade Commission (FTC) regulations can have a network marketing company quickly be put out of business by the regulatory authorities.

Only 4% of Dentists Will Retire Financially Free.
Will YOU Be One Of Them?

Learn How You Can . . .

- Increase Practice Profitability
- Provide Cutting Edge Services To Your Patients
- Create New Profit Centers That Can Add $2,000 To $8,000 Or More Monthly To Your Bottom Line
- Enhance The Image Of Your Practice
- Implement Significant Tax Reduction Strategies
- Develop A Royalty Income That Can Supplement Or Even Surpass Your Professional Income
- Create Quality Free Time To Enjoy Your Wealth

*Dr. Tom Ventullo –
living a life of choice.*

Just a few years ago, Dr. Tom Ventullo was looking for a way to support his patients to be healthier, while increasing his practice profitability. Not only did he add an extra $6,000 per month to his practice income through *The Prosperous Dentist – ABC Co. Profit Centers*, but was able to develop a royalty income with a part time effort that far exceeded his practice income. He is now retired from practice (in his 30's) so he can spend quality time with his family, vacation monthly and coach his son's baseball team. Today, Tom is committed to supporting other dentists to increase their incomes and practice because they *choose to* not because they have to. If financial security and time freedom interest you, call today.

Call
800-999-9999

For More Information

The
Prosperous Dentist
Financial Growth System
. . . committed to your success

Figure 3.7   Dental Products Magazine Display Ad

Direct Mail

Direct mail can be an effective means of introducing your benefit-laden mailing piece to hundreds of thousands of potential customers and prospects. Network marketers have successfully mailed postcards, booklets, letters, flyers, audio and videotapes, CD and DVD ROMs, and self-mailers to their targeted audiences. Similar to placing an ad in a print publication, direct mail success results from a sufficient number of responses

Figure 3.8 Inc. Magazine Ad

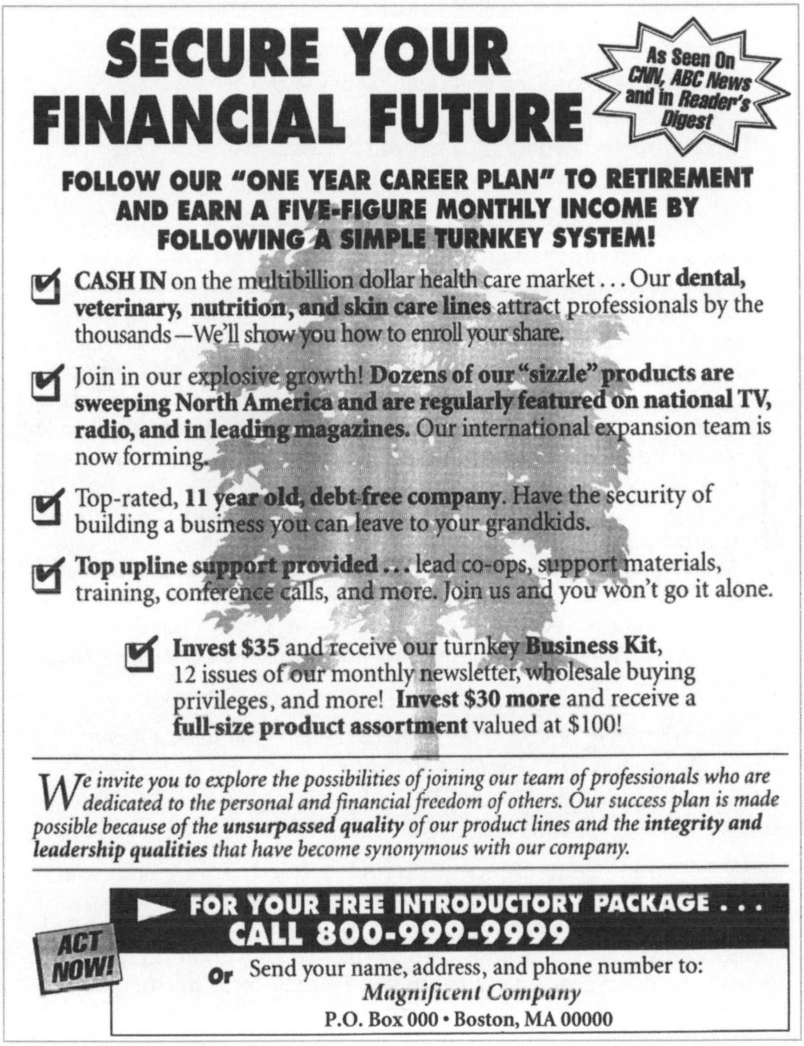

Figure 3.9 Home Business Magazine Display Ad

Are you tired of the same old 9 to 5 rat race?

Sick of not controlling your financial destiny?

Sick and tired of aggravating commutes, long hours, and not being appreciated for the work you do? Well, there is a better way!

The way out of that daily grind called your j-o-b (which, for too many, sadly stands for *just over broke*) is to start your very own, successful home-based business.

In America today, every 11 seconds, someone will start a new home business! And the company that can help you to succeed in launching a lucrative business from home is the Magnificent Company! Since 1984, the Magnificent Company has been supporting tens of thousands of people *just like you* to successfully run a profitable and rewarding business from the comfort of their own homes. The Magnificent Company's products are the very best. In fact, more than 10,000 doctors proudly recommend the Magnificent product line to their patients.

For many, the Magnificent Company's simple, home business system has meant earning enough extra money with a part-time effort to make a new car or house payment. Others have replaced or exceeded their full-time earned income, thanks to their Magnificent business!

> *John Smith of Boston, Massachusetts, says, "It has been a dream come true. After a little more than a year after I started my Mag-nificent business, I was able to retire from my professional position and fully replace my income from home!"*

The Magnificent Company provides full training and every-thing you'll need to help you succeed. You simply use the extraor-dinary Magnificent products, which include about 70 nutritional, weight loss, and personal care products, recommend your fa-vorites to others, and help those you introduce to do the same!

We're so sure that you'll agree that the Magnificent Company of-fers a phenomenal opportunity that can impact your life for the better, just as it has for tens of thousands of others just like you, that we're willing to prove it to you risk free! No catches. No obligation.

Call 800-999-9999 today and request our free brochure. That's 800-999-9999. The call is free and so is the brochure—so don't miss this chance to gain control of your life and your financial fu-ture! Call today: 800-999-9999.

Exhibit 3.1   Sample Radio Commercial

Are you sick of too little money working at a job that offers little personal satisfaction? Sick and tired of aggravating commutes, long hours, and not being appreciated for the work you do? Well, there is a better way!

The way out of that daily grind is to start your very own, successful business by working at home on your computer. If you can send e-mail, you have the skills necessary to learn how to build a life-changing income from home while working at your computer, just by following the Magnificent Company's online turnkey income system.

> *Dr. Tom Jones of Sacramento, California, says, "Working from home on my computer is awesome! I've replaced my full-time income after only two years of working part-time from home!"*

The Magnificent Company provides full training and everything you'll need to help you succeed, including your very own *free* web site and full training on how to build wealth from home. We're so sure that you'll agree that the Magnificent Company offers a phenomenal work-at-home program that can impact your life for the better, just as it has for tens of thousands of other folks just like you, that we're willing to prove it to you risk free! No catches. No obligation.

Call 800-999-9999 today and request our free info package or visit www.Magnificent.com and take a *free* no obligation tour of our system. That's 800-999-9999 or www.Magnificent.com. The call is free and so is the tour, so don't miss this chance to gain control of your life and your financial future! Call today: 800-999-9999 or visit www.Magnificent.com.

Exhibit 3.2   Work-at-Your-Computer Radio Commercial

being generated from any particular mailing. The bottom line for this and other forms of advertising comes down to the ultimate cost and quality of each lead generated. Here are some tips to consider ensuring a successful direct mailing campaign:

- Purchase a fresh, updated list that targets the demographics of your ideal prospects. If the list is a quality one and you purchased it for repeated use, you can mail to it again and again. If you rent the list, you will be restricted to a one-time mailing. The quality of the list will greatly influence the success or failure of your mailing. Do not be tempted to save a few dollars by purchasing or renting a list of questionable value. Make sure the list owner can guarantee the reliability of the names and the correctness of their mailing addresses. Your most rewarding results will come from purchasing a list of people who have recently responded to a similar offer or purchased a similar product by mail. For example, by mailing your pet product offer specifically to pet owners rather than to the general public, your success ratios will improve markedly.
- Do a small test-mailing of between 500 and 1,000 pieces to determine your ultimate cost to generate each lead. Alter various factors such as the ad content, color and size of the mailing piece, ad headline, the call to action, and the target group to which it is mailed to test which changes result in more responses per dollar spent.
- Offer a discount coupon, special incentive, or free item if the prospect or customer responds by a certain deadline. The effectiveness of your mailing will be in direct proportion to the value of the offer you create and the timeliness of the benefits offered.
- Place a hard hitting benefit or direct challenge on the outside of the envelope or mailing piece to create value and

arouse curiosity that will result in your customer reading the offer and then acting on it.

- Expect between a 1 percent and 3 percent response. Make sure that such a rate of response will make your mailing cost-effective. Compare your ultimate cost per customer or prospect to the cost to generate a customer or prospect using a different advertising medium. Consider that the cost of mailing to each 100 names might look something like the following: postage ($37), envelopes and stationery ($12), printing ($12), labor to compile mailing ($8). Your total cost to mail to 100 names might therefore be $69. If your efforts result in the generation of only one customer, will you recoup your $69 with just this one sale? If your efforts result in converting one respondent into a business builder, that would translate into a $69 cost per each new distributor obtained in this fashion. Over the years, I have found that direct mail typically results in a higher cost per acquisition than other advertising methods.

- To increase your rate of response, purchase lists containing phone numbers of people who have requested to receive information on your product type or area of interest. Make sure these names and numbers are not on the FTC's *Do Not Call* registry list or you may be liable for fines up to $11,000 for each violation!

- Rather than mail an expensive item like a CD/DVD ROM or videotape, include a self-addressed return postcard in your mailing that the recipient can drop into the mail to receive the item offered. This will ensure that only interested parties who request your presentation will receive it, saving you thousands of dollars of waste from unwanted items that would only get tossed into the wastebasket.

Flyers, Ad Cards, and Drop Packs

Flyers can be attractively typeset, inexpensively printed on colorful paper, and distributed in a variety of ways. These include placing them on car windows, under apartment and office building doorways, on bulletin boards, and on telephone poles. Ad cards can be placed on pay telephones, in bathroom stalls, and just about any other place that a flyer might be placed. Drop packs typically consist of a flyer, ad card, or brochure secured within a plastic baggie. A small pebble is added to the baggie, allowing the distributor to easily toss it onto a front porch, walkway, or lawn.

A word of caution applies to these methods of advertising. First, make sure that local ordinances permit placing of flyers or distributing packages in this manner. Second, ask yourself if you will generate more anger by placing unwanted clutter and leave an unprofessional impression upon those you expose with this methodology. Lastly, does this method represent the image you wish to convey about your company, products, and opportunity? As you might guess, for the preceding reasons, this is not one of my preferred methods of spreading the word.

The Call-Fax-Call Approach

This approach is a great way to target small business owners who may benefit from your company's product line or income opportunity. It involves three simple steps:

1. Call the small business owner to explain how your company benefits this group. Ask for permission to fax them a one-page sheet outlining the benefits of your program. Ask for the name of the person who would evaluate such a

program. Request permission to follow-up with this person later that day or the next day to answer any questions and inquire about his or her level of interest.

2. Fax your one-page sheet to the attention of the person referred to in Step #1.

3. Follow-up with a phone call to answer questions and gauge interest. Since this approach involves cold calling a list of suspects to determine who will identify themselves as actual prospects, success will result from speaking with sufficient numbers to make this a viable pathway to build your business.

Exhibit 3.3 shows an actual script I've used to target kennel owners with our company's products and income opportunity. Alter it to pertain to your company's program and the niche market you'll target. Exhibit 3.4 shows the fax we would send.

Trade Shows and Conventions

Trade shows present a great opportunity to put your products and income opportunity before literally hundreds or even thousands of prospects, typically during the time span of a day to a week. These shows can range from a small, intimate gathering with a small table space rental costing less than $100 and manned by a single distributor or two to a massive exposition lasting several days that might fill a huge convention center. Booth space at such a show might run up to $10,000 or more and require a co-op agreement among a dozen or more distributors, who share the cost of the space and alternate to provide coverage over the entire run of the show. Those distributors who rent booth space agree to share the product sales and the income opportunity prospects who express an interest.

Hello, my name is _____ and I am calling from _____'s office. To whom am I speaking, please?

(Sally)

Sally, our company is supporting kennel owners to implement significant income streams by showing clients exactly how they can better support their pet's health and be more competitive in races and shows. One of our most in-demand products is the Magnificent Company Pet Nutritional Drink. This product has a track record of supporting animals to be healthier and in better physical condition.

Another of our exceptional products is the Magnificent Company Dental solution. When added to the pet's water bowl, it safely eliminates all bad breath and is about 60 percent as effective as brushing the pet's teeth—and we know how few owners brush their pet's teeth! In addition to being a great benefit to your clients' pets, this program can easily add a significant income stream of several thousand dollars monthly to your kennel's bottom line. It can also provide for a lucrative staff bonus program in which the staff shares in the profits generated.

May I fax you a one-page sheet explaining our program's benefits?

(Yes)

Thank you. To whose attention should I send the fax?

(John Smith)

Great! May I call you tomorrow to see if Mr. Smith has an interest in learning more about the Magnificent Company Pet Care Products and Programs? When would be a good time to reach him?

(or)

May I send you a package detailing the benefits we provide? Who would be the person to evaluate adding this service to your kennel?

(Mr. Jones)

Great! May I set up a time to speak with Mr. Jones and answer his questions, next week after he has had a chance to review our package?

Exhibit 3.3 Telephone Script for Permission to Fax/Send Introductory Letter or Package

---

Pets Love Magnificent Products

For more than a decade, the Magnificent Company has supported thousands of health care professionals and has serviced millions of satisfied patients with their safe, effective, state-of-the-art products and programs. The Magnificent Company Pet Care product line will support your clients' pets to realize optimum health and wellness. The Magnificent Company Program is auxiliary based, easy to implement, and can be incorporated directly into your existing patient base. Let us show you how to add $2,000 or more to your business' bottom line each month!

Some of the high quality Magnificent Company Pet Care products are listed next.

- Pet Dental Solution—Promotes healthy gums, eliminates bad breath, and improves oral hygiene.
- Magnificent Company Pet DeStress—Life-changing ingredients that provide stress relief, improve endurance, support healing, bolster the immune system, and support several other areas of health.
- Magnificent Company Pet Relaxant—Reduces nervous tension and does not reduce alertness.
- Magnificent Company Pet Antioxidant—Enhances mobility and increases vitality in animals.
- Magnificent Company Pet Deodorizer—Powerful, safe, and nontoxic.
- Magnificent Company Pet Ear Cleaner—Used for preventive measures in pets' ears and in conjunction with the professional care of infected ears.
- Magnificent Company Pet Gel—Helps reduce healing time for cuts, burns, hot-spots, and so on.

(Continues)

Exhibit 3.4   Pets Love Magnificent Products (fax)

- Magnificent Company Pet Shampoo—Special formula that is pH-balanced and hypoallergenic with no harsh chemicals.

- Magnificent Company Pet Toothbrush—Compact and flexible, has an independent, patented, triple-head configuration that accommodates a wide range of tooth sizes. Makes brushing a pleasant experience for pets and owners alike.

For a NO-OBLIGATION, free information package just FAX this sheet to us at (800) 999-9999 with the following information:

NAME: _____

FAX#: (_____) _____

ADDRESS: _____

PHONE #: office (_____) _____ eve. (_____) _____

Best Time: _____

Or

Leave a message (toll free) at (888) 999-9999 with your name, number with area code, and a convenient time to speak.

    Thank you!

John Smith
Dr. Tom Jones
www.MagnificentCompany.com

Exhibit 3.4 Pets Love Magnificent Products *(Continued)*

Here's a cover letter to the kennel owner:

Dear Mr. Smith:

The Magnificent Company, a leading distributor of extraordinary pet-care products is now supporting top kennels such as yours with a number of cutting-edge products and income-generating programs. The Magnificent Company pet and health care products are endorsed by thousands of veterinarians, health care professionals, and their staffs throughout the United States and Canada. We are now seeking kennel owners, veterinarians, veterinary technicians, and pet groomers who would like to experience the benefits that the Magnificent Company provides.
We offer:

- A leading edge *Pet Care Line* known for its unsurpassed deodorizing properties as well as for products to support increased mobility, health, and well-being for all animals. The Magnificent Company Pet nutritional drink supports pets to look and feel their best. Many dog kennel and horse stable owners rely on this life-changing product to provide their racers with a significant competitive edge.

- The opportunity to work in partnership with other colleagues in the pet industry, developing a *self-generating royalty income* that could equal or exceed your current professional income.

- The chance to deduct your lifestyle expenses, including many of your current expenses, by taking advantage of the *tax benefits* our business system can provide.

To receive your FREE INFORMATION PACKAGE explaining the Magnificent Company Program benefits for the kennel or stable owner, please call (888) 999-9999.

Of course, there is no obligation.

Yours in health,

Tom Jones
Magnificent Company Marketing Director

Exhibit 3.4 *(Continued)*

Trade shows can range from niche-specific affairs that appeal to a certain profession or group to general business-to-business conventions that target the needs of businesses. They can also be opportunity or product expos open to the general public. These shows cover all interests from auto and boat shows to home and vacation shows and to dog and exotic pet shows as well as thousands of other categories. Some shows even feature home-based business opportunities whereby distributors compete to create value for the prospects in attendance.

Conduct some research to determine if your company's products or services may fit well with the theme of a particular show. Our team members have sold up to $10,000 in products at some of the large pet and dental trade shows where these themes specifically targeted two of our product lines. At some shows, those distributors working the booth split hundreds of quality leads whom they would continue to follow up in the weeks following the show.

Conducting a successful trade show booth depends upon several key components. Here's a list of some proven guidelines to support your success.

- Request a floor plan and booth space layout from the convention coordinator. Select a good location for your booth that will put you where the traffic flow is best. Avoid back rooms and remote, hard-to-find locations. It's often better to pass on accepting a poor location if that's the only space available.
- Determine if your focus for the show will be on selling products or services to attendees, or if you will primarily concentrate on creating interest in your income opportunity. Some shows lend themselves to both possibilities. If this is the case at your show, have a product display at one

end of the booth and an income opportunity presentation at the other. You'll want to convey the fact that the extraordinary nature of your products makes possible your awesome income opportunity.

- Make sure your energy is friendly, upbeat, welcoming, professional, and attractive to convention attendees. Low-energy presentations, sloppy dress, food in the booth, or amateurish displays have no place at successful trade show booths.

- If your intention is to prospect for distributors interested in creating their own home-based businesses—which I strongly suggest you consider doing—I recommend creating an attractive banner or sign that speaks to your income opportunity. Kinkos and other sign makers offer this service.

  Some possible slogans for this sign might be:

  - Where Will YOU Be Financially in 4 Years?
  - Work at Home and Earn What You're Worth
  - Distributors Wanted: Earn a Full-Time Income with a Part-Time Effort
  - Work from Home on Your Computer
  - Partners Wanted for Lucrative Expansion into New England Areas
  - Entrepreneurs Wanted: Share in Our Company's Profits
  - Earn a Dream Income from Home
  - Lose Weight, Make Money
  - Or any other headline that will allow you to create an opening to discuss your income opportunity

- Set up your booth in an open U shape with a table at the rear of the booth. This setup welcomes and encourages attendees to check out your offering instead of keeping them away with a barrier. Place some chairs in your space and invite prospects to make themselves comfortable as you discuss your presentation.

- Have one or more distributors work the aisles, asking a question that arouses curiosity and interest while inviting passersby to learn more about your company, products, and income opportunity. Build rapport, exude warmth, and avoid being pushy or offensive.
- Have a professional video or DVD presentation featuring your products, company, and opportunity running continuously. Set up this presentation on the side of the booth that features information about your income opportunity.
- Next to the video presentation, have a book filled with satisfied customers' testimonials and successful business builders' stories.
- Offer a drawing for a free product or some other valuable prize in exchange for attendees filling out a brief survey card that lists name, address, e-mail address, phone number, and their level of interest (1 to 10) in either products or income opportunity. Invite attendees to sign your guest register to receive additional information.
- Inform attendees that your company offers superior products that make the awesome income opportunity possible. Briefly explain the top products' most important benefits. Say that your business is growing rapidly and you are interviewing for associates to join your team. Offer those who express a significant interest (7 to 10 on your rating scale) a free package consisting of a cover letter containing your story, a product catalog, and a prospecting brochure. If your company has an inexpensive audiotape, CD, or DVD explaining the income opportunity, include that as well. For those who express a lesser interest, offer a one-page fact and testimonial sheet

explaining the most important benefits of your products, company, and opportunity. Always include an e-mail address, web site URL, and business card in all of your prospecting packages.

- If your booth is equipped with Internet access, set up a notebook computer that features your company's web site. If the booth does not have an Internet connection, download to your desktop about 5 to 10 of the most important web pages and display them for all to see.

- Make sure your booth, signage, prospecting materials, and setup all communicate a professional and successful image. Avoid handwritten or unprofessional appearing signs, table drapes, and other elements.

- If a small, separate meeting room is available for your use in the convention facility, use it to conduct powerful but brief (approximately 12 minute) overviews scheduled every 30 to 60 minutes. If a room is not available, arrange a number of chairs to the side of your booth, if space allows, and conduct your presentation right there. Have all distributors working the booth invite everyone to attend the next informative lecture. Have your most effective speaker conduct these presentations. Have her begin by taking two minutes to share her story, including how and why she was initially introduced and attracted to the company and income opportunity.

    Next, take two minutes to explain about the network marketing industry, establishing its longevity and speaking to bolster its credibility with your prospects. Take another three minutes to briefly explain the benefits of your product line and another five minutes to demonstrate a success model that illustrates how geometric progression works. Underscore the value of creating a residual or royalty-type income.

I like to show a model depicting how identifying and partnering with 4 business builders will result in a sizable organization. These 4 identify 4 others, who identify 4 others, who identify 4 others. This model of 4/16/64/256 creates a total of 340 people—all using and recommending $100 in products per month. It generates $34,000 in total organizational sales, which if commissionable at 30 percent, yields a residual income of $10,000 or more each month. You'll need to apply your own company's compensation numbers to such a model.

Ask for a few testimonials on the products and income opportunity if other distributors are present at the meeting. End with a call to action—requesting the names and contact information of those who would like to learn more. Inform the group that you are available to answer any questions, or speak privately to anyone who expresses an interest.

- Make interested prospects a valuable offer. It may sound like this: "If you decide to join our team today by becoming a distributor for the Magnificent Company and place your first product order, we will commit to supporting you to get off to a great start. The next business builder we identify today who is interested in joining our team will be placed in your organization. What's more, we will make this same offer to this distributor and to their new distributor and so forth down the line! So, you could actually end the trade show with a solid line of business builders in *your* very own group, just for having the foresight to get started today." Create excitement and convey a sense of urgency by rewarding those who are ready to commit to their own success.
- Research other trade shows that will take place in the coming three months. Have a sign-up sheet and take commitments to reserve additional booth space so that

you can build momentum from show to show. This tells prospects that you are committed to supporting them to share in the success that such a pathway allows.

- Commit to following up all the leads generated, within the next week or two after the show. The longer you take to re-establish contact, the less likely will you be to rekindle the interest sparked at the show.
- Don't pass up your chance to develop rapport with other booth owners. These entrepreneurial individuals are often looking for additional income opportunities or products to add to their current booth offerings. Network with other presenters, sending people their way when possible. Your thoughtfulness will be rewarded tenfold.

Professional Business Receptions

Professional business receptions or PBRs are a great way to build your business with velocity by using your and your prospects' and team members' circles of influence. PBRs are typically hosted in a home or office until such time that the numbers attending expand to require a hotel meeting room or function facility. Even with limited numbers, they can be successfully conducted in a home or office by inviting guests to come, have fun, and learn about your company's products and income opportunity. Here are some keys to hosting a successful professional business reception.

- Hold your PBR in a comfortable setting. A home's living room or office boardroom is perfect.
- You'll need to invite five people to get at least one to attend. Encourage your team to each commit to bringing at least one or two prospects with them.

- Have the senior leader serve as the master of cere-
monies. The person hosting the PBR should introduce
the senior leader with a powerful introduction that establishes credibility.
- Serve tea, coffee, or soft drinks but never alcohol. It's critical that you create a professional atmosphere conducive
to a business presentation. If your company sells a shake,
drink, or food product, have samples available for your
guests.
- Here's a format that works well.

  - If your company has a well-done video or DVD presentation, play that first.
  - After viewing this, have the host introduce your senior
leader to conduct the presentation. As with any powerful presentation, he or she should edify the speaker,
point out his or her accomplishments, and tell a hu-
morous or interesting story that endears the speaker to
the group.
  - The speaker will begin by sharing his or her story,
telling how and why they became involved with your
company. This story should be inspirational and convey his or her vision, which the Magnificent Company will make possible. It should also contain a
pledge of support to all present to work with the new
people joining the team to achieve *their* own personal
success.
  - The speaker should establish the credibility of the network marketing concept and explain the value of creating a residual income.
  - He should also explain the asset value of such an income. (You would need to tie up $1 million invested at
4 percent interest to create a monthly residual income

of $3,300. Point out how much easier it is to build an organization that will pay you this amount.)

- The speaker should then establish the credibility of the company, outline the benefits of the product line, and establish their value in making the extraordinary income opportunity possible.

- He or she can show a model demonstrating how geometric progression works to build wealth (4 who get 4, etc.) and end with a call-to-action challenge to join the team.

- He can also extend an invitation to connect with the person who invited each guest to discuss building his or her own network marketing dynasty.

- The entire presentation should take no more than 20 to 30 minutes before opening up the conversation for questions. The evening should end with casual conversation about the company, products, and opportunity as coffee, tea, soft drinks, or dessert is served.

- For those prospects interested in getting started right away, plans can be made to schedule and host additional PBRs to support their business-building efforts.

- Unless you can be assured of gathering enough prospects and team members to fill a large hotel or function-hall meeting room, it is better to first host your meetings in an informal setting like a home or office. A meeting with 10 new prospects attending can look like a great success when held in a home but a terrible, disappointing failure when held in a hotel meeting room.

- Use the PBR format to build locally. It is an especially effective means for people with significant warm market contacts to build their businesses. It also does not necessitate the need for additional lead generation expense.

Lead Lists

Today, numerous lead generation companies offer lists of opportunity seekers or work-at-home prospects. These lists often come with name, mailing address, phone number, and e-mail address. Some also include a brief survey filled out by the prospect to describe his level of interest.

The quality and cost of these lists can vary tremendously. Often, the higher priced leads may be fresher, may be sold exclusively to one or two clients, and may contain a survey filled out describing the prospect's interest. Some are also pre-qualified by phone to make sure that the prospect is, in fact, still interested in evaluating a home-based business opportunity. Beware that the quality of a leads list is not always proportionate to the cost. Many unscrupulous vendors resell the same worthless lists multiple times to unsuspecting buyers.

Moreover, leads can be gathered by a number of different methods. The lowest-quality leads may have registered for a free drawing, lotto, or other perk—meaning that they probably are not serious prospects. Opt-out leads are also of poor quality. These people are considered prospects unless they remove themselves from the lead pool. Obviously, many people fail to take action to clarify their real status so that they, too, are misrepresented as a lead when they are not interested in any opportunity. Leads harvested by co-registration methods whereby the person may not have read the fine print saying they agree to be contacted for a business opportunity, are also typically of very poor quality.

Opt-in leads are those who have agreed to receive information about a home-based business opportunity. Again, not all opt-in leads are serious prospects. Some will not even remember filling out an opt-in request. Double opt-in leads are screened twice, giving the prospect two chances of opting out if desired. More qualified leads are those who actually responded to an advertisement closely resembling what your opportunity offers. Some companies promise to sell these leads exclusively to one buyer for a certain time period, typically two to four weeks. Again, leads that have been prequalified by calling to verify the accuracy of their information, while confirming their interest, are usually the best bets.

As most lead lists today are compiled from Internet ads, all reputable companies will offer a verification and date the lead was generated proving that the person actually responded to an offer. This verification is important proof to avoid being accused of spamming or worse, calling someone who has registered their name on the national Do Not Call registry. Again, a word of warning: Violating this request can result in up to an $11,000 fine per incident. For safety reasons, some companies actually mark those names that are *not* on the DNC list, thus providing a great measure of safety and peace of mind in following up only those people who wish to be called.

The best way to determine which type of leads is most productive for your purposes is to test a batch of each. By tracking your success ratios, you can identify if you are better off purchasing more inexpensive leads or fewer, more costly ones. For example, one inexpensive lead company I tested generated a ratio of two enrollments per 100 names. These leads cost $60 per 100, so the final cost to acquire a distributor translated to be $30 each. I conducted another test in which I purchased 20 $5 leads for the same cost of $100. These generated two new distributors as well. The difference between these two lists turned out to be the time I needed to call each prospect. In the end, although the final cost per new distributor worked out to be the same dollar amount, I subsequently opted to purchase more of the better, more expensive leads as they required less total prospecting hours to generate a similar result.

Internet Auto-Responder Systems

Many network marketing companies and a number of service companies have created generic systems designed to serve the networking industry to automate the prospecting process online. These companies have created various online business-building systems that perform the following functions:

- Introduce prospects to the network marketing concept with online movies, text, and audio programs.
- E-mail a series of messages that go out on a set schedule automatically via auto-responder to opt-in prospects who have agreed to receive offers regarding a home-based business opportunity.
- Introduce prospects to the network marketing company with which they are affiliated and its product line and income opportunity.
- Continue to drip on prospects by sending as many as 100 different e-mail messages inviting them to find out more and to try a sample product order.

These systems can be very effective in sifting through lead lists to identify interested prospects. In all systems, an e-mail message serves as an initial contact, sparking interest and beginning the prospect's educational process. They do *not* take the place of personal phone contact. They do *not* eliminate the need to build rapport and do *not* replace the partnership, relationship, and leadership elements that are so critical in building a thriving network marketing dynasty.

(Subject line) **Turn Your Computer into a Money-Making Machine**

Our fully automated online wealth building system makes building a lifetime royalty income a stress-free, simple process.

If you can send e-mails, you can build an income just by inviting others to visit our site. The site explains exactly how anyone can build wealth simply by inviting others to visit the site and follow the system.

We're so sure our system will make you money that we're willing to GUARANTEE your success!

Simply visit www.MagnificentCo.com, take a FREE tour of our system and within 28 days, you'll have a ready-to-go organization in place. If you don't agree that it's the simplest way ever developed to build wealth at home, you'll be under no obligation and will have incurred no cost to test its effectiveness for 28 days.

Just by taking the free tour of this incredible system, you'll lock in your spot and be in a position to secure an online income. We will e-mail you every time we place another person in your contact group.

Remember, it's FREE to see just how effective our system is in creating potentially lifelong wealth. No credit card or payment is needed. The tour will show you just how simple building wealth from home can be.

Visit www.MagnificentCo.com and lock in your position now!

Exhibit 3.5 Message #1

(Subject line) **Our Company will pay out $200 million in 2005.**

Part of it could be YOURS!

Work at home on your computer and share in the wealth. We are a **21-year-old company** that has supported people just like you to build wealth from home. We will do $200 million more in sales the next year, showing people how to use our Online System to **create personal freedom** from home.

If you can read this and know how to send an e-mail, then you are more than qualified to **start earning a weekly income right away**.

We will **teach** you how within a few minutes. The best part is you can try our system for **FREE** by starting right now.

To begin learning how you can earn money right away, please visit www.MagnificentCo.com and take a free tour of our fully automated system. **We look forward to working with you and supporting your success.**

Exhibit 3.6   Message #2

Exhibits 3.5 through 3.8 are a series of e-mail auto-responder messages we have used successfully to mail to opt-in lists of opportunity seekers. You'll need to adapt them to describe your own company's opportunity.

Press Releases and Publicists

Press releases can be used as an effective way to introduce your company's new product, service, brochure, video, impending event, promotion, or other newsworthy event.

We GUARANTEE You a Downline!
And We'll Prove It for Free BEFORE You Join!

With Our Automated Online System, If You Can Send E-mails, You Can Make Money!

Let Us Prove It to You for Free!

Step #1: Visit www.MagnificentCo.com.

Step #2: Take a FREE tour by entering your name and e-mail address.

Step #3: Receive FREE details by e-mail explaining EXACTLY how this system works to make you money.

Step #4: Share Your Very Own FREE Personalized Web Site Link with Others to Show Them Exactly How THEY Can Also Make Money.

Step #5: Receive FREE Training Explaining How To Succeed Just by Sending People to Your Site and Directing Them to Us to Show Them How To Build Wealth with Our System!

You have nothing to lose and everything to gain!

Visit www.MagnificentCo.com now and take the FREE tour! E-mail me at MAGNIFICENTCOMPANY@def.com.

Exhibit 3.7   Message #3

Because they are not advertisements, they inherently convey third party credibility in a manner that informs rather than sells.

Many magazines, journals, and newspapers will accept and publish press releases as a courtesy to their readers. At the same time, these releases are often used to fill empty

(Subject line) **Every company pays somebody . . . We pay you!**

This wealth-building concept makes more sense than any other business model ever created either on- or offline! You earn money for doing what you already do but currently are not getting paid for doing:

Recommending and promoting!

We all do it. When we find a restaurant we really loved or a movie we really enjoyed, we tell everyone we see how great our experience was. The result? People go and see the movie or try out the restaurant.

Do you get paid for recommending and promoting the restaurant and movie? Certainly not!

Would you like to get paid for recommending and promoting things to friends, family, and associates . . . or on the Internet? Why not?

We've introduced a totally automated online system that recommends and promotes products and services to interested buyers. All you have to do is send e-mails to people interested in earning some extra money (and we have even automated that!).

This system is totally FREE to try out. Prove to yourself that you can earn money BEFORE YOU SPEND EVEN ONE CENT! Click here to find out more and take a FREE tour of the system: www.MagnificentCo.com.

Exhibit 3.8   Message #4

space in the publication. It is not uncommon for publications that sell advertising space to agree to publish your company's press releases as a thank-you for patronizing their magazine or newspaper.

Effective press releases announce newsworthy product introductions, events, or stories. They are easy to read, informative, and to the point. It is often wise to include your most important points, web site URL, and contact information early in the release, in case the editors shorten its content to fit in with their space requirements.

To secure placement of your release, you can either contact your target publication directly or use a wire service to expose your release to a wide range of print publications and other mediums. To do it yourself, send your release via mail, e-mail, or fax to the publication's appropriate editor along with a photo of the product, company, or person featured. The *Gale Directory of Publications and Broadcast Media* is a great resource for newspapers and their editors. You can find a copy at your local library. Here is a listing of press associations arranged by state:

State Press Associations

> Alabama Press Association http://www.alabamapress.org/
> Arizona Newspapers Association http://www.ananews.com
> Arkansas Press Association http://www.arkpress.org/
> California Newspaper Publishers Association http://www
>   .cnpa.com/
> Colorado Press Association http://newmedia.colorado
>   .edu/cpa/online/
> Florida Press Association http://www.flpress.com/
> Georgia Press Association http://www.gapress.org/
> Idaho Newspaper Association http://www.idahopapers.com/
> Illinois Press Association http://www.il-press.com/

Inland Press Association http://www.inlandpress.org/

Northern Illinois Newspaper Association http://www.star
.niu.edu/nina/

Hoosier State Press Association http://www.hspa.com/

Iowa Press Association http://www.inanews.com/home1
.html

Kansas Press Association http://www.kspress.com/

Kentucky Press Association http://www.kypress.com/main
.html

Louisiana Press Association http://www.lapress.com/

Maine Press Association http://www.mainepress.org/

Maryland-Delaware-D.C. Press Association http://www
.mddcpress.com/

Massachusetts Press Association http://www.nepa.org
/about.html

New England Newspaper Association http://www.nenews
.org/

New England Press Association http://www.nepa.org/

Michigan Press Association http://www.michiganpress
.org/indexb.shtml

Minnesota Newspaper Association http://www
.mnnewspapernet.org/

Mississippi Press Association http://www.mspress.org/

Missouri Press Association http://www.mopress.com/

Montana Newspaper Association
http://www.townnews.com/

Nebraska Press Association http://www.nebpress.com/

Nevada Press Association http://www.nevadapress.com

New Jersey Press Association http://www.njpa.org/

New York Newspaper Publishers Association
http://www.nynpa.com/

New York Press Association
http://www.nynewspapers.com/

North Carolina Press Association http://www.ncpress.com
North Dakota Newspaper Association
    http://www.ndna.com/
Ohio Newspaper Association http://www.ohionews.org/
Oklahoma Press Association http://www.okpress.com
Oregon Newspaper Publishers Association
    http://www.orenews.com/
Pennsylvania Newspaper Publishers Association
    http://www.pa-newspaper.org/
South Carolina Press Association http://www.scpress.org/
South Dakota Newspaper Association
    http://sdna.com
Southern Newspaper Publishers Association http://www
    .snpa.org/
Tennessee Press Association http://www.tntoday.com/
Texas Community Newspapers Association http://www
    .txcommunitynewspapers.com/
Texas Daily Newspaper Association http://www.tdna.
    org/
Texas Press Association http://www.texaspress.com/
Utah Press Association http://www.utahpress.com/
Virginia Press Association http://www.vpa.net/index.htm

One service that will send your press release to thousands of U.S. editors instantly is *Business Wire*, www.business wire.com. It's the standard in the industry. The fee for this service is typically between $300 and $500. Another free service, though much less effective is *News Wire*, www.prweb.com. Companies who will distribute press releases via the Internet to the media are *Internet News Bureau*, www.newsbureau.com and *URL Wire*, www.urlwire.com, which accepts online related material exclusively. *Advance PR* will send your press release out to 10,000 media sources,

---

For Immediate Release
Dental Instruction Brochure Now Available

The Magnificent Company announces the introduction of a
new *Dental Instruction Brochure*, explaining in simple-to-
understand language exactly how patients can practice
proper oral health and fresh breath maintenance through
simple oral hygiene procedures that include irrigation,
tongue scraping, brushing, flossing, rinsing, and application
of a topical gel, using the components found in the **Magnificent Company Hygiene Kit**. To request your **FREE brochure
and sample Hygiene Kit**, call 800-999-9999 or E-mail: mag-
nificentco@aol.com.

Magnificent Company
P.O. Box 000   Boston, MA 00000

Figure 3.10   Sample Press Release

www.pressreleases.net. *Internet Wire* is another reputable Internet service, www.internetwire.com.

Figures 3.10 through 3.13 are some examples of press
releases I have used effectively, with names altered to insure impartiality. The use of press releases, though not typically a standalone business-building strategy, can be an
effective means of generating high quality customer and
prospect leads.

Publicists

Publicists are individuals hired to acquire publicity for a company, product line, or individual. The cost to engage the services of a publicist can range from several hundred dollars to

---

For Immediate Release
Opportunities for Educational Professionals
Audiotape Now Available

The Magnificent Company announces the introduction of a FREE audiocassette tape entitled *Opportunities for Educational Professionals*, explaining how to increase your net income without working more hours. Topics covered include how to:

• Add new office income streams.

• Create a value-added client-centered approach.

• Differentiate your business with easy-to-implement "customer-magnet" services.

• Supplement your income through additional profit-generating opportunities.

To request your free booklet, call 800-999-9999 or e-mail MagnificentCompany@mail.com

  Magnificent Company
  P.O. Box 000   Boston, MA 00000

Figure 3.11   Sample Press Release

$10,000 or more each month. Publicists typically take on only clients with newsworthy products or announcements. Most contract for a minimum time commitment of at least three months. Some publicists have great radio and television contacts while others specialize in print media. Publicists prefer to represent book authors, famous television, movie, sports, or political personalities or companies with announcements possessing significant public interest. Before hiring a

The Magnificent Company announces the introduction of its new Professional Tooth-Whitening System. The kit consists of the following:

- 1 oz. 19% Carbamide Peroxide Gel in an easy-to-use accordion dispenser (more product than is offered by most other whitening systems in an easier-to-use format)
- Travel-size, Magnificent toothpaste which is low in abrasion, effective in cleaning and deodorizing the mouth and a great adjunct to the system
- Tooth Whitening Shade Guide
- 2 Vacuform Resin Sheets for custom trays
- Tray container

The fresh mint-flavored Magnificent Whitening gel is hydrated and has a neutral pH to minimize sensitivity and viscous to enhance its ability to maintain contact with the teeth. This system joins the comprehensive Magnificent oral health line recommended by thousands of leading dentists throughout the U.S.A. and Canada.

A 30-patient no-risk clinical product trial is offered along with bulk rebates and FREE product bonuses of up to $500. For more details or to arrange a NO-RISK clinical trial, call 800-999-9999 or e-mail MagnificentCompany@aol.com.

Figure 3.12   New Product Release

publicist, ask for references from companies offering similar products or services who have utilized the publicist's services with good results. Consider asking for a guaranteed minimum commitment of media exposures before hiring one.

As you can see, there are a myriad of lead sources and prospecting pathways that can guide you to building your ul-

---

For Immediate Release

The Magnificent Company announces the promotion of Susan Jones of Littletown, Maine, to the position of National Sales Manager. Ms. Jones is a graduate of ABC College and originally hails from the town of Hope, Idaho. Ms. Jones was awarded her promotion along with a check for $50,000 to acknowledge her rise to the Magnificent Company's top sales position. The Magnificent Company reports that Ms. Jones is currently accepting applications for sales positions in all 50 states. To contact Ms. Jones to receive a free information package describing the Magnificent Company's offerings, call 800-999-9999 or e-mail MC@aol.com.

Figure 3.13   Sample Press Release

tra-successful network marketing dynasty. It is not important that every distributor be able to work every particular method of building available in order to be successful. It takes only finding at least one way that works for you. Some distributors will be extremely effective at cold calling. Others, like me, prefer to place ads and reply to those who express an interest. Some like hosting professional business receptions and so forth. Encourage your team to find the pathways and prospect sources that allow them to maximize their own personal effectiveness and productivity. There's usually a way that works for every distributor—if she possesses the commitment to keep working until she finds it and then masters this approach.

Now that we've thoroughly discussed how to generate enough leads through a variety of methods, let's examine how to create a prospecting system to support the success of new and seasoned distributors alike.

ESTABLISHING A SIMPLE, DUPLICABLE PROSPECTING SYSTEM

Successful prospecting systems typically share a number of common characteristics.

1. They are duplicable. Most anyone can immediately follow the system and experience enrollment success, which is not reserved exclusively for only the company's most charismatic master presenters. The systems put into place make the presentation for the distributor. His or her job is as simple as connecting the prospect to the system.
2. They are professionally produced and communicate quality, longevity, and success. Poorly written or worn out copies of letters or flyers and amateurish audiotapes or web sites have no place in a duplicable system intended to convey an image of success.
3. They are inexpensive to acquire and use and are made readily available to new distributors, especially those on a limited budget.

Let's now examine some possible components of such an effective prospecting system.

1. A brief prerecorded toll-free opportunity message available 24/7. This sort of message can serve as an integral part of any successful prospecting system. New distributors can three-way call their prospects to listen to this short overview of the company, products, and opportunity. This type of message does a far superior job of explaining the benefits of associating with your company than a new distributor could initially hope to do by himself.

2. A three-way call or teleconference presentation. After listening to the message, if the prospect expresses an interest in learning more, the new distributor can simply arrange for another three-way call with his sponsor or success-line mentor, or he could tie the prospect into a company or success-line sponsored income opportunity group teleconference presentation.

Please see the accompanying text box for a sample opportunity call script that can be recorded by either a company officer or successful field leader. If your company or success-line does not offer this type of brief toll-free overview, adapt this script to your opportunity or simply create your own.

Toll-Free Opportunity Recording

Hello and thank you for calling this brief overview presentation of The Magnificent Company. My name is Joe Jones and I've been with the Magnificent Company for 10 years. I am a top income earner and serve as a member of the President's Inner Circle. My association with The Magnificent Company has been truly life-changing. Ten years ago I was working at a dead-end job in a shoe factory, earning minimum wage. After four years of part-time effort with the Magnificent Company, I was earning an exciting professional income that made possible the realization of many of my wildest dreams. These included retiring at the age of thirty-five, paying off all my debt, buying the house of my dreams mortgage-free, and having the money to travel around the world at least six times a year with my wife and children.

The Magnificent Company has been in business since 1983 with a record of supporting tens of thousands of

(Continues)

Toll-Free Opportunity Recording *(Continued)*

people just like you and me to create successful home-based businesses. Our company pays lucrative income bonuses to those who spread the good word about our wonderful products and our exciting income opportunity. Success is as simple as using our products, recommending your favorites to others, and sponsoring people who want to earn an extra income. We enjoy an unsurpassed reputation for integrity in company and field leadership while offering the finest personal care products available. We are represented by hundreds of thousands of successful associates doing business in every state in the U.S.A. and every province in Canada.

Our products have received widespread acclaim and countless favorable publicity in such leading publications as *Redbook*, *McCall's*, *Shape*, *Seventeen*, and *Family Circle Magazine*. Our company president, Mr. Tom Thomas has been interviewed by *Forbes* magazine and has appeared as a guest of Larry King and Oprah Winfrey.

Because of the efficacy of our unique and extraordinary products, we have supported thousands of associates to create life-changing home businesses. The best part is that we have only just begun to grow! Our greatest growth clearly lies in our future. In fact, we expect to grow four-fold in size in the next two years. So you couldn't have picked a better time to join us. Our successful associates earn anywhere from a small extra income of a few hundred dollars monthly, maybe enough for a nice new car payment, to significantly more, like a few thousand monthly, maybe for a beautiful new home payment, to an exciting six-figure professional income that allows many to retire early and pursue a life of choice, rather than work at a job that no longer provides satisfaction, simply because they have to put food on the table. Of course, what you earn will depend upon the efforts *you* put forth.

> **Toll-Free Opportunity Recording (Continued)**
>
> Our associates can demonstrate for you our simple yet effective turnkey system designed to champion your success. Please get with the person who invited you to listen to this overview and ask them to show you EXACTLY what it would take for you to earn a life-changing income with the Magnificent Company. We look forward to partnering with you toward your success.

Duplicable Distributor Web Sites

Most network marketing companies offer a very professional corporate web site for their distributors' use. Many of these same companies have the capability of cloning this site for personalization by all distributors. By offering this feature, distributors can add their own personal photos, story, and introductory paragraphs to create value, develop rapport, and educate web site visitors. These duplicable web sites are often included in the cost of becoming a distributor or are available for a small monthly fee, which covers the costs of keeping the site current and adding any desired features to support distributors to manage their business growth, order products, and effectively communicate with their organizations. One great benefit of such a duplicable web site is the ability for all distributors to convey a professional image from day one while offering their prospects this same ability, if they decide to join the team. An additional advantage is that by controlling site content, companies avoid the risk of irresponsible therapeutic and income claims made by distributors that could result in the Food and Drug Administration (FDA) or the FTC shutting down the company for legal violations, thus placing everyone's financial future in jeopardy.

Personalized distributor–corporate web sites serve as a great free or inexpensive tool to use to build your business. It's easy to send a link to everyone you know, requesting that they check out your company and opportunity. Your web address can be included in all ads you place as well as on your stationery, business cards, and signature file.

When prospecting a person who agrees to take a look at your company, products, and opportunity, ask if he has easy access to the Internet. If the answer is yes, suggest he visit your web site (along with listening to your company's prerecorded message) before speaking with you for your scheduled follow-up call or meeting. Doing so will save you the expense of mailing out a prospecting package before prequalifying recipients. If your prospect likes what he sees on your site, you can always follow up with a traditional package containing a catalog, prospecting brochure, and audio or video presentation.

Generic Network Marketing Web Sites for Prospecting Opportunity Seekers Online

A number of companies offer to distributors affiliated with any network marketing company a duplicable, personalized web site that can be used to screen hundreds or thousands of leads who have opted in to receive information on a home-based business while working on the computer. These web sites typically offer videos to educate online visitors about the benefits of creating a home-based business while enticing them to explore what life might be like if money were no object and they could actually realize their fondest dreams.

Many of these generic systems do a good job of explaining the network marketing concept and the value of creating a residual income. They are effective in sorting through large numbers of inexpensive online leads to identify the serious prospects in the group. Distributors involved with companies that do not offer the duplicable web site option can take advantage of these sites to communicate a professional business-building system to support the value of the networking concept. Many such companies also offer a wide array of customizable auto-responders to drip on the hundreds, thousands, or tens of thousands of leads that can be easily entered into their fully automated system. Some examples of companies offering such a program are www.iprodirect.com, www.growthpro.com, or www.wtpowers.net.

Although these automated web site systems complete with lead e-mailing capabilities can be a nice way to sift through the masses of uninterested parties in search of the serious prospects, they best serve as only a first step in the prospecting process. Personal contact with the prospects who want to learn more through a phone conversation complete with rapport building, partnershipping, and team-building support are critical elements necessary for building a network marketing dynasty.

Using Your Company's Support Materials

Even in this modern day and age, approximately 25 percent or more of your prospects will not have easy access to the Internet or will be computer-challenged to some degree. Many also prefer the ability to hold a brochure or book in their hands, listen to an audiotape on the way to work, or watch a video or DVD presentation in the comfort of their favorite easy chair. For these prospects, it is important to have a ready supply of professional support materials that explain your company's history and vision, the value of the product line, and the life-changing possibilities made available through the income opportunity. Because some prospects are visually oriented while others learn better through auditory means, it is usually a good idea to include some written material in each prospecting pack along with an audio or video presentation if available.

Prepare these packs ahead of time. Include a business card and have a blank piece of stationery in each so that you can hand-write a personal note at a moment's notice. Keep some packs handy in your car and some at home and work. Successful networkers often keep a pack or two in a large handbag or briefcase, always ready to pass it along to a receptive prospect when the opportunity arises.

For prospects new to the concept of network marketing, also be sure to include a generic educational tool explaining the value of the network marketing concept. *Brilliant Compensation* by Tim Sales or *Mailbox Money* by Richard Brooke work well for this purpose.

Let's now turn our attention to the arena of what to say to our prospects to increase the likelihood of successful enrollments.

Matching Your Situation While Addressing Your Prospect's Needs

What you will say to your prospects will depend upon a number of factors. These include how well you know the prospect, how much rapport and relationship you have established to create an opening for him to be interested in listening to what you have to share, and where you'd guess his interest may lie. Obviously, your presentation will differ if you are speaking to your Uncle Charlie, someone who has answered a display ad you placed in a targeted niche publication, or the lady standing in line next to you at the supermarket checkout line. In spite of these varying situations, all successful prospecting conversations will share a number of common elements.

Let's look at these three situations in greater detail to see how a typical prospecting conversation might go.

First, in the case of speaking with someone you know fairly well, there are a number of ways to create an opening to share about your company, products, and income opportunity.

Here are some opening lines you might say to a person you already know.

- Uncle Charlie, I've recently partnered with some very successful business leaders to support our company's expansion into the Chicago area. I admire your business expertise and thought I'd ask if you'd consider taking a look at what we're doing with an eye toward possibly joining me as a business partner.
- Uncle Charlie, I know how health conscious you are. I'm working with a company that distributes some exceptional nutritional supplements. Would you be willing to take a look at them and let me know what you think? I'd appreciate you becoming a customer if possible. Thanks!
- Uncle Charlie, I need your help. I'm leading my company's expansion into New England, and I'm looking for some potential business partners. Would you be willing to give me 30 minutes so we might brainstorm who you think might be willing to take a look at what we're doing?
- Uncle Charlie, I'm looking to partner with a (your uncle's occupation) to introduce our company's product line to this group. Would you be interested in exploring some possible synergies with me?
- Uncle Charlie, who do you know who could use some extra money?

Here is something you might say to someone who answers an advertisement.

- Hello, is Linda there? Hi, my name is Joe Jones and I'm returning your call. You left a message after seeing our ad in the *Boston Globe*. Is this a good time to visit for a few minutes? Great! Before I tell you about our company and income opportunity, would you please tell me a little about yourself? Where do you live, what do you do for a living, and what sparked your interest in our ad?

Here are some things you might say to someone whom you meet as you go about your day.

- Hi, I think I've seen you before in this store, shopping. I was wondering if you might be able to give me some advice. I'm new to the area and looking for people who might want to earn some extra income from home, working with a very well-respected multimillion dollar company. Would you possibly know of anyone who might be interested in an interview? If so, I could arrange it so that our company would send you a nice thank-you check for your referral.
- Break the ice and develop rapport by speaking about something that sparks your attention. It could be as simple as commenting on the weather or a newspaper headline at a newsstand, complimenting someone on her jewelry, and so on. Follow up this small talk with a compliment and a question that creates an opening. For example, you might say, "You look like the kind of professional person I'm looking for. Would you be willing to listen to this audiotape? I'd be happy to touch base with you after-

ward to see if you'd like to learn more. Would that work for you?"

- Use an elevator presentation. Thanks to Hilton Johnson of MLM University for this technique. Break the ice. Develop rapport. Say something like, "You look familiar. Do you work around here?" (Yes) "Oh, what do you do for a living?" When they answer, say something like, "Really, I'm looking for people like you in my business." If they ask you what you do, say something like, "You know how (fill in the blank). Well, what I do is (fill in the blank to create an opening)."

Here are some examples:

You know how most people work all their lives earning less than they really deserve, only to retire and be forced to live on half of what was too little to begin with? Well, what I do is show people how to retire 15 years earlier at twice their usual pay level. Do you know anyone who might be interested in learning more about that?

You know how most people work all their lives at jobs that don't pay them what they're worth? Well, what I do is show people how to get paid what they're worth by doing what they love to do! Would that interest you to learn more? What day this week can we talk for a few minutes?

You know how companies pay huge amounts to advertise their product lines? Well, what I do is show people how to get their share of these revenues. Our partners earn up to a high six-figure yearly income. Do you know anyone who might be interested in learning more? We're interviewing right now for self-starters interested in getting paid what they're worth.

Of course, having a simple system in place will dramatically support you and your new distributors to achieve great success. For example, if you or your company has in place that brief five-minute company, products, and income opportunity toll-free message I discussed earlier, all you'd have to do is say something like, "Would you have just five minutes to listen to a brief summary of what I do to support people to earn extra money from home?" If the answer is yes, use three-way calling to connect your prospect to the recorded message. Or if you are out and about town, hand her your cell phone to listen in. After she has heard the message, ask if your prospect would be willing to further explore this possibility of making money from home. Make a request that your prospect take a next step. This might mean speaking with your business partner, attending a meeting, trying an initial product package, watching a video, and so on.

Let's now look at Exhibits 3.9 through 3.13, some sample scripts I use to follow up interested prospects who have responded to an advertisement. You'll need to adapt the script to fit in with your company, product line, and compensation structure. Remember that any script serves as a starting point rather than a word-for-word rigid presentation that you must read and follow to the letter. Become so familiar with your script's flow that you can alter it, as needed, to guide your prospects along in learning about your offering. Always develop rapport and create rich possibilities for them as you go.

Exhibit 3.14 on page 130 is one more sample conversation script that you may wish to internalize as a guide to support your prospecting conversations. This is a script our team uses to follow up advertising leads that have been acquired online. The key to success with calling leads of this type is to follow up at least six times (via phone and e-mail) until you get a "yes, no, or keep me on a mailing list and try me later."

You: Hello, this is Joe Jones. May I please speak with Jane?

Phone Answerer: Who's calling?

You: This is Joe Jones with the work-at-home program, returning Jane's request for information on our program.

Phone Answerer: Yes, just a minute, please.

Prospect: Hi, this is Jane.

You: Hi, Jane, this is Joe Jones with the work-at-home program. I'm calling in response to your request for information on how you can earn money from home by working on your computer. Do you have a few minutes for me to explain how our simple, fully-automated program is supporting people to develop exciting incomes working at home on their computers?

Prospect: Yes, I have a few minutes.

You: Great. People are joining our program by the thousands every week. These range from some who are looking for a few extra hundred dollars each week to others working a plan to build a high six-figure yearly income, and many somewhere in between. Can I ask you a few questions before I explain how the program works to see where there might be the best fit?

Prospect: Sure.

You: Thank you. First, can you tell me a little bit about yourself, who you are, what you do, why you are interested in working at home? In other words, anything that will help me to know you better and to better understand what is important to you so I can see if there might be a fit with what we do.

(Develop rapport and make a friend.)

(Continues)

Exhibit 3.9 Script for Following Up "Work at Home on Your Computer" Business Opportunity-Seeker Leads

Also, if you looked back on this day in a year or two, from an income perspective, what would make your decision to join us in partnership worthwhile? Would you be interested in earning a little extra income, like a few extra hundred a month—maybe enough for a nice new car payment? Or maybe a few extra thousand a month—like enough for a nice house payment? Or are you interested in establishing a full-time professional income by working part-time from home—like many on our team who have retired early, thanks to our program, which has produced financial freedom for them?

Prospect: As much as possible. $10,000 a month would be great.

You: Great. I can show you *exactly* how you can earn that type of income.
    Can I tell you a little about our program?

Prospect: Please do.

You: We are partnered with a well-established multimillion dollar international corporation that has been supporting people just like you and me to create life-changing incomes for the past 21 years. Our company is called the Magnificent Company. Have you heard of us?

Prospect: I think my doctor has recommended the Magnificent Company's products.

You: Yes, thousands of leading health care professionals have been recommending the Magnificent Company's products to their patients since 1984. I'm sure you'll agree the Magnificent Company products are the finest available anywhere. We offer about 70 different products including oral health care, personal care, nutritional care, weight-loss, air-purification, and pet care products.

Exhibit 3.9 Script for Following Up "Work at Home on Your Computer" Business Opportunity-Seeker Leads *(Continued)*

But not only do we offer the finest products that people use and recommend to others every day, but our new, fully-automated online wealth-building system is allowing people to create exciting incomes online just by sending others to visit our web site and test-drive our income-generating system for free. We simply invite others to visit our web site. This includes both people we know, like those in our address books , and those, like you, who have answered an ad about working at home.

When they visit the site, they can test-drive our system and prove how easy it is to earn thank-you money from the Magnificent Company just by inviting others to visit the site and check it out. Since the test drive is free, there's absolutely nothing to lose. In fact, within a few days, you will see that people are already joining your organization.

You will be creating your success as you and others spread the word and invite people to visit the site and see for themselves. It works great. It's a simple, explosive way to build wealth from home. Do you have a pen handy so I can give you my web address, allowing you to register for free without cost or obligation to check it out? This way you can see how simple it is to get started toward building a nice check from the comfort of your home.

Prospect: Sure, I'm ready.

You: Great. Simply visit www.mywebsite.com and enter your name and e-mail address. You'll receive free details showing you exactly how you can be successful in building wealth from home. Also, do you have a few more minutes so that you might listen in to a short message from Tom Smith, the Magnificent Company's CEO?

Prospect: Sure.

You: Okay, please hold one moment.

(Continues)

Exhibit 3.9   *(Continued)*

(Three-way your prospect into the five-minute opportunity call at 800-999-9999.)

After listening to the prerecorded presentation:

You: Do you have any questions, so far?

(Answer any questions your prospect has or three-way her with your success-line partner to get her questions answered.)

Prospect: No, not now.

You: Very good, Jane. Can we set up a time when we can speak, in a day or two after you've visited the site to see how well the system works, so I can answer any questions you might have?

Prospect: Okay, that sounds great.

You: Would Thursday at 8 P.M. Eastern time work for you?

Prospect: Yes, that should work just fine.

You: Great! I'll call you at this same number, 978-999-9999 on Thursday at 8 P.M. Jane, my promise to you is, should you decide to join our team, I will partner directly with you and be fully committed to your success. Jane, if for any reason, should you be unable to keep our appointment, would you please call my toll-free number at 888-999-9090 to let me know at least 24 hours before our call? This will allow me to offer this time to someone else.

Prospect: Yes, I'll be happy to do that.

You: Thank you for your time and interest. Have a great evening.

Exhibit 3.9 Script for Following Up "Work at Home on Your Computer" Business Opportunity-Seeker Leads *(Continued)*

Step 1: Place ad.

Double your practice income by showing patients just how healthy (or not) they really are. Determine their precise nutritional needs with our simple, revealing test. For FREE information and Sample Test Report, call 800-999-9999.

Step 2: Call, using this prospecting script specifically for targeting chiropractors:

Hello, my name is Bill Bean and I am calling from Dr. Sponsor's office. To whom am I speaking, please?

(Sally)

Sally, our company is supporting chiropractors to implement an individualized nutritional testing protocol in their practices that will show patients exactly how healthy they are—or not. Our test is designed to demonstrate specific nutritional needs and deficiencies, as it measures more than 70 key components, the health of 13 different organs, the presence or absence of 8 toxic metals, and much more.

In addition to being of great benefit to your patients in specifically addressing their nutritional needs and potential challenges, this program can easily add a significant profit center of several thousand dollars monthly to your practice's bottom line. It can also provide for a lucrative staff bonus program allowing you and others in your office to share in the profits generated.

May I fax you a one-page sheet explaining our program's benefits? To whose attention should I send the fax?

(Dr. Smith)

Great! May I call you tomorrow to see if Dr. Smith has an interest in learning more about the Magnificent Company Nutritional Program after she has reviewed the fax? When would be a good time to reach the doctor?

(or)

May I send you a package detailing the benefits we provide as well as a sample test for your practice to evaluate? Who would be the person who would evaluate adding this service to your practice?

(Dr. Jones)

Great! May I set up a time to speak with Dr. Jones and answer his questions next week after he has had a chance to review our package?

Step 3: After obtaining permission, send the chiropractic fax in Exhibit 3.11.

Exhibit 3.10 Steps for Successfully Prospecting Chiropractors

**Contributing to Patient Health
& Practice Profit Centers!**
*Analyze Your Patients' Nutritional Needs and Add
$50,000 Yearly or More to Your Practice Bottom Line!*

For more than a decade, the Magnificent Company has supported thousands of health care professionals and has serviced
millions of satisfied patients with their safe, effective, state-of-
the-art products and programs. The Magnificent Nutritional
Test and Product Line will support your patients to clearly identify their body's precise, individual nutritional needs and deficiencies. The Magnificent Program is auxiliary based, easy to
implement and can be incorporated directly into your existing
patient base.

Here are some of the benefits of the *Magnificent Program*:

- **A convenient, cost-effective home analysis test kit** that includes everything needed for submitting a specimen, including a self-mailer. The test targets the patient's specific
  nutritional needs and deficiencies and measures more than
  70 key components, the health of 13 different organs, pH al-
  kalinity, and the presence or absence of 8 toxic metals!
- **An independent lab** conducts the analysis and returns to the
  patient a detailed, beautifully illustrated 38-page booklet describing the exact findings of the test and what they mean
  specifically to educate patients about their nutritional needs
  and challenges. Similar testing offered by 85% of U.S. and
  Canadian hospitals typically costs $750 or more!
- Based upon the test's findings, a **specific nutritional plan** is
  then recommended by the chiropractic professional addressing the patient's needs. Targeted Magnificent nutritional
  products are then recommended and provided by the practice as an extraordinary health-centered service.
- All of these structured programs provide your practice with
  monthly profits ranging from $50–$300 per patient! By supporting your patients to best understand and address their

Exhibit 3.11   Chiropractic Fax

exact nutritional needs, a **lucrative office profit center** is created which can also allow for a **rewarding staff profit-sharing program**.

- An optional **Colleague Referral Program** can allow for the creation of an unlimited royalty income by introducing other health professionals to this and similar programs. Two to four years of part-time effort can provide you with a permanent "full-time" income. Ask us for all the details.

For a NO-OBLIGATION, free information package, just do one of two things:

1. Fill out and FAX this form to us at 800-999-9999.

   NAME: _____

   FAX#: _____

   ADDRESS: _____

   PHONE #: office (   ) _____ evening (   ) _____

   Best Time _____

OR

2. Leave a message at 1-800-999-9999. Be sure to leave your name, number with area code, and specify a convenient time to talk. We look forward to being of service to your patients and your practice.

THANK YOU!

Yours in health,
Your Name
Your Dr. Partner's name

Exhibit 3.11 *(Continued)*

Thank you for calling. If you would like to add an extra income stream to your life this year, we can help. We are a group of very successful health and business professionals who are committed to supporting people just like you to earn an income that will have a significant impact on the quality of life. Because of our ability to show people exactly how they can achieve financial freedom, we were featured on the cover of *Success* magazine and in their cover story, "We Create Millionaires, How Network Marketing's Entrepreneurial Elite Are Building Fortunes at Breakneck Speed." Please allow me to share with you who I am and how we can support you to achieve wealth through our simple, proven system.

(Share your company's publicity or facts to support credibility.)

My name is Dr. Joe Jones. I'm a leading distributor and Master Instructor for the Magnificent Company. For the past 15 years, I've been helping people just like you to create financial success. Thousands of people throughout the United States, Canada, and Asia credit their success to the wealth-building systems we have put into place. And now it's your turn.

I'd like to send you some free information about our company, the Magnificent Company and the wealth-building program that has supported tens of thousands of folks to develop an income that has impacted their lives. Our program is simple, it's powerful, and most importantly, it really works. We'd like to show you how you can earn streams of extra income immediately. And the best part is this: My associate and I are willing to coach you to succeed for free, if you are ready to take action and join us in partnership.

The Magnificent Company has been supporting people to achieve financial success since 1984. The Magnificent Com-

Exhibit 3.12   Prerecorded 24/7 Toll-Free Message for Gathering Advertising Leads

pany product line is extraordinary and consists of many unique "sizzle products" recommended by thousands of health professionals to hundreds of thousands of their patients. We enjoy a great reputation for leadership and ethics while championing people to develop life-changing incomes.

Are you ready to change your life? Are you ready to allow us to coach you to financial success? If you can answer yes to the following three questions, you're the type of person we are looking for.

Question 1: Would you be willing to spend 5 to 10 hours a week working with me and our team, following our proven *7-Step Success System* if you could really be successful at this?

Question 2: As you know, it can sometimes take thousands of dollars to launch a new business from scratch. However, you can get started with our system for about $100–$300. And of course, all of our products are extraordinary and fully satisfaction guaranteed. In fact we have several sizzle products that people MUST have, when they learn about them! Is your financial freedom important enough that you would be willing to commit such a small amount of money to get started?

Question 3: On a scale from 1 to 10, with 1 being I'm just window shopping and 10 meaning I'm extremely interested, how would you rate your interest level at this time?

If your interest level is at least a 6, we invite you to leave your name, address, phone number, and e-mail address, if you have one, so we can send you valuable free information. Due to the tremendous response we receive, we can provide you with information only if you are willing to leave a phone number.

If you are interested in making a decision that can be absolutely life-changing, please leave your name, address, telephone and e-mail address (if you have one) at the sound of the tone, and we'll get you all of the details.

Exhibit 3.12 *(Continued)*

The advertisement reads:

> Stay-At-Home Moms Needed, Earn $500–$1,000 a Month From Home. Full Training Provided. CALL 555-555-5555 for a FREE Info Packet.

The voice mail message says:

> You have reached the Magnificent Company home office of Dr. Dennis Pezzolesi. I'm sorry I am currently unavailable to come to the phone. Your message is very important to me. If you are replying to an ad, kindly leave your name and phone number and specify the best time range for me to call you back. I look forward to speaking with you soon.

Here's the script:

1. *Get their attention:*

   Hi, Mary, this is Dennis Pezzolesi. You answered an ad I placed in the *Rare Reminder* for stay-at-home moms. I'm just getting back to you at your request. Do you have a few minutes to speak now?

2. *State the facts:*

   I'm calling to ask what you are interested in before I send out information about our program. This is not a job. It's a home-based income opportunity. Is that of interest to you in learning more about it?

3. *Listen to the story:*

   Most prospects will want to hear what you have to offer at this point. It's important for you to learn about their story, develop rapport, and get into their world.

4. *What is this?* They will eventually get to the point of asking you what you are introducing to them. Direct the conversation to address their needs and wants. Here's what I say:

   I'm with a company called the Magnificent Company. We have been in business for more than 20 years. I've personally been with this great company for 11 years.

Here's where I tell my story. After that, I get back to what it is:

> The Magnificent Company is a network marketing company. Are you familiar with this concept? (Most are not.) Well, there are

Exhibit 3.13 Stay-at-Home Mom Script
(Thanks to Dr. Dennis Pezzolesi for sharing this one.)

three ways to earn income with our company. First is retail income. That means selling products for a profit. You may choose to do this only or to not do this at all. Most successful income earners do this to some extent. When you discover how truly awesome our company's products are, you'll naturally think of people who will want to try them and keep buying them from you, since they are consumable products that everyone needs. This does two things for you: It builds income and creates security.

I then tell them briefly about our product lines and offer a story if I see an opening regarding how any of the products relate to my prospect.

Mary, the next way you will get paid from the Magnificent Company is with bonuses. You see, the company rewards those who enroll others who place orders for our products. This is especially lucrative if you know anyone who may have an outlet for our products. [Give a few examples of occupations that have done well with the Magnificent Company.] Also, when someone wants to build an income with the Magnificent Company, they order an initial product mix called a quick-start order. You can earn up to $200 on each one of these orders. These are paid daily! This leads me to the third way to get paid with our company and that involves residual income. Are you familiar with the concept of residual or royalty income, Mary? Well, it's like writing a book, or acting in a movie. Once you do it, you get paid on it for life! I'll explain more about how to build such an income with our company when we speak again next.

5. *What's my role:*

Mary, my responsibility in all of this is to support you to develop an action plan to create the income you desire. I will also work with you initially to carry it out. You see, you'll be in business for yourself but not by yourself. I also want to let you know that you will be eligible for great tax savings by establishing a home business. We can discuss this aspect in more detail when we get together to formulate your action plan.

Address your prospect's questions and concerns before you send her an information pack. Send your story letter, a prospecting brochure, and a product catalog. Set a follow-up date to speak within 24 hours after your prospect receives this packet.

Exhibit 3.13   *(Continued)*

Hi. My name is Tom Thomas and you were referred to me because you responded to an Internet advertisement. I understand you are interested in creating income from home with a home-based business. Is this a good time to visit with you for a few minutes? Great!

(If no, schedule a time to speak.)

I represent a very successful multimillion dollar company named the Magnificent Company. Have you heard of us?

(If yes, ask what they know about the Magnificent Company.)

(If no)

We have been successfully supporting people to create life-changing incomes at home since 1984. In fact, our group is more than 110,000 strong and we have hundreds joining us every day because of the simple, duplicable success system we have in place.

Before I explain a little about our company, products, and success system, is it okay if I ask you a few questions to get to know you better to see if there may be a fit for you?

(Sure.)

Great! Thank you.

Can you please tell me a little about yourself, what you are looking for in terms of a home business (if you know), and what level of income monthly would make a home business worthwhile for you?

(Ask further questions to develop rapport and get into the prospect's world. Say things like, "Tell me more about that. How long have you been doing that for a living? Have you lived there long?" Build the relationship and make a friend.)

Can you tell me what caused you to reply to the ad? We offer the opportunity to earn anywhere from a little extra income monthly (like a car payment or house payment) to the ability to replace a full-time income. For others, we represent a chance to achieve great wealth. We do this by following a simple business plan that I will explain in a minute. What type of income monthly are you looking to achieve?

Exhibit 3.14 Sample Conversation Script

(Any income amount)

Great! I can show you *exactly* how you can earn that much and more.

Allow me to tell you a little bit about our company, products, and home-business opportunity. We have partnered with an international multimillion dollar company named the Magnificent Company to support people just like you to create life-impacting incomes. We are a twenty-one-year-old company with an outstanding reputation for extraordinary products and for supporting people to develop an income that can be life-changing. Have you heard of our great products? We have five product lines. Our dental care line is recommended by tens of thousands of dentists and hygienists to their patients daily. We also have extraordinary weight loss and nutritional product lines.

In addition to the oral health care and nutritional lines, we have a unique pet care line. Our hottest product in this line is the Magnificent Company Pet Solution. When added to the pet's water bowl, it totally eliminates bad breath and at the same time is about 60 percent as effective as brushing any pet's teeth. We find that no one wants to brush their pet's teeth daily. Do you have any pets or know anyone who does?

The Magnificent Company also has a line of great personal care products that people use every day. In addition we have an air purification line that is great at eliminating all odors including pet odors, smoke, and smoking odors. It's a godsend for folks with allergies and asthma.

In a nutshell, the Magnificent Company offers a wide variety of exceptional products that people love to use and recommend.

The Magnificent Company's products are marketed through network marketing. Are you familiar with network marketing?

(If no)

Instead of putting its money into an advertising budget, the Magnificent Company has chosen to pay lucrative bonuses to those who use and recommend their products and business opportunity.

(Continues)

Exhibit 3.14 *(Continued)*

(If yes)

Great! Have you ever been involved with a network marketing company before?

What was your experience like? Let me show you an example of how you could earn a nice monthly income from the Magnificent Company by doing 3 key things:

1. Use the Magnificent Company products and identify your favorites.
2. Recommend these Magnificent products *and* the Magnificent business opportunity to others (just as I am doing now) and
3. Sponsor those into your Magnificent Company business who want to earn some extra money, whether that is a little extra income or enough to retire early on and do what you want to do when you want to do it.

In the plan I'm about to demonstrate, let's assume that you and I work in partnership to identify and support four other people to use and recommend the Magnificent products and business opportunity. For example, do you know anyone who could use some extra money? What is that person's name?

(Tim)

Great! What does Tim do for a living?

(Tim is a teacher.)

Teachers are wonderful in this business. Do you think Tim knows some other teachers who could use some extra money?

(Sure, don't all teachers need extra money?)

Absolutely! Okay, do you know anyone who might be interested in shedding some unwanted pounds?

(Yes. Sue.)

And what does Sue do?

(She is a stay-at-home mom.)

Perfect. Sue must know other stay-at-home moms or moms who wish they could stay at home. Don't you think?

Exhibit 3.14 Sample Conversation Script *(Continued)*

(Definitely!)

(Continue to leap-frog your prospect until she gets the idea of how easy it is to come up with names of people who may be interested. For more on the technique of leap-frogging, see the next section.)

Please put your name at the top of a page and the number 4 under it. We will identify and support 4 others to use the products, recommend the products and the business opportunity, and sponsor others in need of some extra money. That gives us:

You
+4 more

We will also partner to support these 4 to do the same thing—to use the products, recommend the products and income opportunity, and sponsor at least 4 others in need of some extra money. We now have:

You
4
16

We will partner with our 4 as well as their 4 to support these 4 to do the same thing—to use the products, recommend the products and the opportunity, and sponsor at least 4 others in need of some extra money. We now have:

You

4
16
64

These 64 also do the same thing—use the products, recommend the products and the opportunity, and sponsor at least 4 others in need of some extra money. We now have:

You
4
16
64
256

(Continues)

Exhibit 3.14 *(Continued)*

Adding these up, 4 + 16 + 64 + 256, we get 340 people, all building a Magnificent Company business. Of all these people, you identified and introduced only 4! When these 340 people each use and/or recommend $100 of the Magnificent Company's products, replacing inferior products that they already are using with superior Magnificent products, you will receive a monthly commission check of about $10,000!

Does that make sense? Do you have any questions about that or anything else we discussed? How does that sound to you so far?

(If your prospect would like more information, ask:)

Do you have access to the Internet?

(If yes)

Please visit www.MagnificentCo.com/yoursite to learn more about the company, products, and opportunity.

(If no)

No problem. May I send you a package that better explains what our company, products, and opportunity are all about?

I'd also love for you to meet my business partner. (Tell a little bit about your partner to edify him or her.) We are part of the Magnificent Company's leading organization. We have an entire support structure to ensure your success.

If you are ready to join us, let's get you registered with the company so that they will know where to send your checks. Let's also set up a call so that I can walk you through our simple, duplicable 7-Step business-building system. Would this Thursday evening work well for you?

Exhibit 3.14 Sample Conversation Script *(Continued)*

Remember, this script will be most effective if you can make it sound like it is a part of you, not something you are reading. Make a friend, have fun, project a successful posture, create value and rich possibilities, and look to contribute to the person. Put yourself in their shoes and speak to them in a friendly, conversational tone.

Take the prospect through the 7-Step Success System, outlined in this book, with your sponsor or success-line partner, if you are not yet ready to do so alone. Always end each conversation with a request that will better support your prospect to move closer to the next step that you perceive will be of interest to them.

If they are familiar with the concept of network marketing, stress:

- Your company's sizzle products
- Your compensation plan, which has people earning several thousand dollars in their first few months in the business
- Your 7-Step Success System, which will virtually guarantee their success if they follow it exactly

You want your prospect to leave the call thinking, "This person is successful and committed to my success! He really cares about helping me be successful. If I join him and follow the system, I will succeed."

A Few More Words about Leap-Frogging

Leap-frogging is an effective technique to support your prospects in realizing that they already know a bunch of people who would be perfect for building a business. Using this technique allows you to bypass your prospects' objections that they don't know anyone who would want to do this while showing them that they do know others who will be able to succeed in building a large group.

I like to go over four leap-frogging examples with my prospects, since my intention is to show that they can be ultra-successful by finding just four people who will also go on to find their four, and so forth. I suggest taking your prospects through four different occupations to ask whom they know who fits this description. For example, I might say, "Who do you know who(m) . . ."

- Needs some extra money?
- Is entrepreneurial?
- You respect and with whom you'd like to be in business?
- Is a realtor?
- Is a chiropractor?
- Is a dentist?
- Owns a pet?
- Wants to retire early?
- Hates their job?
- Would love to stay home with their kids instead of having to put them in day-care?
- Would love to travel more?
- Is great with people?
- Is in the military or retired military?
- Is involved in sales?
- And so forth.

Remember to ask such questions that would bring to mind individuals you think your prospect might know. When they answer, "Yes," say something like, "What's the person's name? What do they do? Where do they live? How well do you know them?"

Confirm for your prospect that the person they mention would likely know others who share this same common characteristic and would likely be perfect for their business. Say, "If you can get them to speak with me briefly, I'll put them into your business for you!" Continue in this manner until you have successfully demonstrated that it's not necessarily just the people your prospect knows but also those individuals *those* people know who will serve their business success.

It's now time for us to look in detail at the elements that will support effective prospecting conversations.

Step 4: Enrolling—
The Power to Enroll: How to Become an Enrollment Machine

The only way to have a friend is to be one.
—**Ralph Waldo Emerson**

How is it that some network marketing distributors can enroll a very high percentage of their prospects while other distributors struggle with little results to show for their efforts? The answer lies in creating sufficient value so that the prospect understands the significance of the opportunity you are presenting and therefore wants to take part in it. While some distributors naturally possess the ability to create rich value, the good news is that anyone can develop these skills by concentrating on the areas I discuss in this chapter.

As I've mentioned, when first introduced to network marketing in 1991, I possessed few enrollment skills. My nervousness caused me to talk *at* people and dump information on them. By doing so, I had no idea about what their world was like, what was important to them or missing in their lives, and how I might contribute to them with my opportunity. Needless to say, my early efforts yielded minimal results. Rather than become discouraged, I decided to reinvent my approach so as to create rich possibilities and extreme value for my prospects. In doing so, I began to pay attention to how I came across to them.

By enhancing your own personal effectiveness, communication skills, and your charisma factor, you will dramatically impact how others perceive your opportunity. In order to build a network marketing dynasty, there are essentially two critical areas upon which to focus. The first is massive and consistent action, persistently following up on all your prospects in a timely manner. The second is to create value and rich possibilities as you communicate to others the gift embodied by your income opportunity.

Recall that massive action is best supported by *a daily action commitment,* namely a promise you make to yourself to speak with a certain minimum number of people each and every day. Initially your conversations will be predominantly prospecting conversations, introducing others to your company, products, and most importantly, to your income opportunity.

As you fill your pipeline with enough prospects, you'll want to add timely follow-up conversations to support your prospects in their evaluation of your opportunity. For some, it will be a fit. For others, it will not. Remember to always ask those who are not interested if they would be willing to support you by becoming a product customer. Also ask if they would suggest a few other individuals who might be open to evaluating your opportunity. When you ask, in this way, for three to five referral names, many of your prospects will be happy to oblige. For those who see the value and agree to get started, you'll need to start training them, either individually or as part of a group. Depending upon their proximity to you, this training can be conducted in person or via telephone.

THE GOLDEN RULES OF
ENROLLMENT SUCCESS

Remember, your ultimate success depends not on how well you can make others do what you want them to do but on how effectively you can identify ways to contribute to their lives. With this in mind,

1. Give up your right to force anyone to do anything just because you want him or her to do it. Sales pressure, begging, and coercion are of little value in this business. You may get some to sign up just to get you off their backs, but if they are to build a business long-term, they must possess self-motivation. Beggars are also not very attractive as business partners, so you'll want to always maintain a posture that communicates: "I'd love to have you join our team but I am not attached to your doing so."

2. Look to contribute value to your prospects' lives. After hearing your presentation, do your prospects know that you are currently or will soon be successful in this business and if they join you, *they* will be as well? If you do your job correctly, your prospect should be thinking, "This must be my lucky day!" After all, it is a true gift you are sharing with your prospects and it would be a privilege for any prospect to have someone as committed as you for a business partner and sponsor!

Let's look closer at some conversational goals upon which you might focus.

Create True Value

Enrollment success depends upon creating great value for your prospects. Is your intention to have your prospects realize that you are offering them some very exciting possibilities to explore? You may want to first check your own belief level. Is your belief rock solid and unshakable with regard to the network marketing concept? Are you proud of what you do or might you be ashamed to some degree of being affiliated with a marketing technique that many mistakenly confuse with a pyramid scheme? Do you confidently see your company as a vehicle to long-term prosperity and economic freedom for at least the next 50 years? Are you absolutely convinced of the value of your products? Are you totally sure that you will be successful and that you know exactly how to support others to be successful? If the answer to any of these questions is not resoundingly affirmative, your prospect is probably sensing that something is missing for you as well. You may be saying the right words but your energy may give away your uncertainty.

The best way to handle any lacking belief is to become convinced of the value of each aspect affecting your offering. Research the network marketing industry. Be able to distinguish the great companies possessing integrity and the ability to impact people's lives from the sleazy schemes that won't be around a few years from now. Be sure your company fits all the criteria of a company you can be proud to represent. Get to know your product line inside and out. Learn and experience the reasons it is extraordinary and worthy of your highest recommendation. Know that the income opportunity is totally sound. Speak with others who have achieved different degrees of financial freedom, thanks to your opportunity. When you are so sure that you made the right choice, you will convey that belief to others through the energy you put forth.

Discover What It Is Like in Your Prospect's World

FLOP them! Ask about their family, where they live, their occupations, and passions or hobbies. Be genuinely concerned about who they are and what makes them special. Offer a sincere acknowledgment if appropriate. Make a friend. When you take the time to build the bond before sharing your information, your prospects will be more likely to listen to what you have to say.

Identify What Is Important to Your Prospects or Missing in Their Lives

How can you hope to understand what would be of interest to your prospects if you have not taken the time to find out what matters most to them? Where is there pain in their lives? What's missing in terms of money, security, fun, fulfillment, or freedom? How might your opportunity address any missing element?

A good way to gain insight into what might matter most to your prospect is to ask, "If money were no object, how would your life be different from what it is today? Would you still continue to work where you are working now? Would you retire early or pursue a hobby or special interest? Would you buy a new car or house? Would you pay off any debt or buy any toys? Would you live where you currently do or move somewhere else? How would you be able to impact your family's lives differently? Would you travel or play more than you presently do? What would change as a result of the financial freedom you had created?" By getting your prospect to dream a bit, you will gain insight into the areas that would make this a game worth playing for them.

Develop a Bond Based on Mutuality and Look to Contribute to Them in Some Way

People like to work and associate with others who share things in common with them. The more areas of interest your prospect shares with you, the more likely he is to like you, trust you, and want to be with you.

If you also can identify some ways that your income opportunity might contribute to him or how your products might be a fit, you will be that much closer to developing yet another thing in common: your business.

With insight regarding some areas in which your offering could contribute to your prospect's life, you can now make a suggestion or request to support him in taking the next step in the evaluation process. Such a request must be in your prospect's best interest, not just in yours! He must be able to understand your motivation for making the request. He must trust that you have his best interests at heart, because you've taken the time to get to know what they are.

Let's now take a look at how we might weave the preceding conversational goals into our discussion to maximize our effectiveness in the enrollment process.

THE FIVE-STEP PROCESS FOR MAXIMIZING YOUR CONVERSATIONAL EFFECTIVENESS

I learned to effectively direct my prospecting conversations by paying attention to the following five steps. In conversations where I covered all five areas, my enrollment success increased dramatically. Conversely, if any of the five steps was missing, the quality of the conversation suffered. I suggest you write these steps down on an index card and have them handy by your telephone to ensure that your conversations cover each of these critical areas.

Step 1: Create an opening to be heard. We create an opening to be heard by first listening to others. We do so as we build the rapport characteristic of the friendshipping process. As we make a friend, we establish an atmosphere of trust. We explore areas we have in common, thus building mutuality.

Perhaps the first step in getting a conversation off to a good start is to be respectful of the other person's time. Always ask if you are calling at a convenient time or if she would be better served to reschedule your conversation. Break the ice by first speaking about something you can identify about the person. Perhaps it is where she lives. You're from Maine and she's from California. Maybe you'll make a comment about how great it is today that technology allows people to be successful partners on opposite coasts. Comment on how you'd love to be able to have a reason to visit California, especially during those cold and snowy New England winters. It really doesn't matter what you talk about—just look for something to set a friendly, conversational tone that supports your prospect to feel at ease.

Step 2: Determine if your prospect is open to exploring if there may be a fit with what you do by getting permission to ask him a few questions. Do this before discussing your income opportunity with him. By asking permission, you lower the prospect's defenses as you ask those questions that will allow you to better understand his world. I might say, "John, before I explain about our company, products, and income opportunity, would it be all right if I asked you a few questions to get to know you better so that I might better be able to look with you to see if there may be a fit for you with what we do?"

Upon receiving this permission, I might ask a second follow-up series of questions. "Can you please tell me a little bit about yourself? Where do you live and with whom? What do you do for a living? What do you like to do in your free time, like on weekends and holidays?"

A talkative prospect may take such an invitation to tell you all about his life story. You welcome this chance by asking follow-up questions and looking for areas of commonality while further developing rapport. For more reserved prospects, you may have to hone in on an easy opening question. You might say, "Where do you live now and have you always lived there?" As your prospect answers one easy question, it sets the stage for you to ask another. Loosen up the conversational mood as you build further rapport.

This line of questioning allows you to listen for what's working in your prospect's life and what's missing. What areas hold the seeds of discontent that could serve as openings to explore how your offering might contribute? A subsequent area that I like to ask about is, "Tell me about your reasons for wanting to explore an income opportunity." Or alternatively, "Let's say after learning about our company, products, and opportunity, you decide to join our team. Let's further say that we decide to partner together to achieve your great success in the next two or three years. How much money would you need to be earning after that time, on a monthly basis, in order to look back upon this day as the day when you made one of the best decisions of your life?" This question establishes the income level that would make your opportunity worthwhile for your prospect. It also tells him that you'll be working in partnership with him to support his success. It thus creates a positive expectation for achievement. It also sets up the next logical question, "How would this level of income impact your life? What would be different for you and your family if you were earning this kind of money monthly?" From there, you're equipped with plenty of reasons to begin exploring your income opportunity.

Step 3: Speak your commitment to your prospect in some way. You want your prospect to realize that she will not need to go it alone to become successful. In fact, you'll be there, by her side, to champion her every step of the way. By speaking your commitment to look without pressure or expectation on your part, you offer to explore if this would be something that would contribute to her life. Voicing your commitment to support her success by working hand-in-hand with her, while showing her exactly what it will take to be successful and then partnering with her in every way to make it happen, reinforces this pledge. This includes speaking to her prospects with her, training her and them, and coaching her team to achieve success. For many serious prospects, such a commitment should be a hard offer to turn down.

Step 4: Create rich possibilities that inspire action. As we have already discussed, it is our job to create value for our prospects. We will actually get paid in proportion to how well we accomplish this objective. When our prospects see a fit for the benefits we offer, believe they can accomplish their goals with our support, and are left with a positive expectation for their success, they will be inspired to get started and to take action.

Step 5: End by making a request that moves the conversation in a forward direction. Requests are the tools that enable us to direct a conversation to a powerful conclusion. You know the value of your company's offerings and what steps will best support your prospect to discover them. Most prospects will not know what to look for or where to get information to make an informed decision regarding whether your opportunity may have value for their lives. It's your responsibility to direct them to see the value. Do this by offering suggestions and making requests.

To increase the chance that your prospect will comply with your request, consider the following key components to a powerful request:

- Your request must be in alignment with your prospects' needs, wants, and desires. It can't be just about you, to make you money, or to only serve your needs. Speak the reasons for your request to help your prospect understand why the action you are suggesting is in her best interests. You might say something like, "Jane, I understand that it is important to you to be able to send your sons to the finest colleges. I know exactly how you can earn enough money to send both of them all four years. Would you be available some night this week to speak with my business partner? She's assisted many people just like you to create lucrative incomes from home." By explaining your motivation for making a request, you've given your prospect insight into why you'd like her to take a particular action. You've pointed out what's in it for her.
- Your request should have a timeline attached to it. Offer a choice of days for a next call. Ask if your prospect can watch a video by this Sunday night. When you put a time frame on your request, you ensure that it just doesn't hang out there indefinitely. Contrast this with a request to just "watch a video." Without specifying a "by when," you have no idea how long it may take your prospect to get around to it.
- Get confirmations from your prospect regarding your requests. With any request, your prospect has the option of either accepting or declining your request. He also may wish to let you know his answer at a later time. Or he may counter-offer with a reply that works better for him. For

example, you say, "John, would you be willing to speak with my business partner on Tuesday night?"

John might reply:

Sure, let's set up the call. 8 P.M. works best for me.

No, I'm not interested in speaking with anyone at this time.

I'm not sure what my schedule is like this week. Can I get back to you on Sunday to let you know if that day will work?

I can't make Tuesday but Thursday will work for me.

Your job is to look for a way that you can support your prospect to take the next step, in a way that works for him. During every conversation you have, ask yourself, "What request can I make that will support my prospect to take the next step? How can I create value for him to appreciate the request? How can I make the situation work well for everyone involved?"

I assure you that if you take on these five steps to guide your prospecting conversations, while paying attention to the conversational goals we discussed, you will see your success ratios improve because more and more prospects will be able to see the same value you see. By doing so, they will decide to take action on your request because it is clearly in their best interests to do so.

Step 5: TRAINING—
TRAIN LIKE A MASTER INSTRUCTOR:
STRUCTURES FOR SUCCESSFUL PARTNERSHIPS

A man should first direct himself in the way he should go.
Only then should he instruct others.

—Buddha

DUPLICATING YOUR SUCCESS
WITH EFFECTIVE TRAINING

You're in massive action. You've become adept at the art of enrollment. New team members are showing up, regularly wishing to take you up on your offer to support their success. So let's look at what training structures you can put into place to facilitate their advancement.

At first, you may have lots of time available to train your new distributors to become familiar with all the products and go through the 7-Step Success System outlined in this book. However, as your business grows and you have new partners showing up who require your support on a regular basis, you'll be well served to put some structures into place to champion their success. If your company offers these structures, commit to utilizing as many of them as possible while stressing their importance to those who join your team. If your company does not, get with your success-line partners and put together your own structure. After all, it's up to you to

151

put into place whatever is needed to facilitate the success of your team.

Company or Organizationally Sponsored Teleconference Opportunity and Training Calls

Many network marketing companies corporately sponsor daily or weekly opportunity and training calls. In those instances where there are no such company-supported calls, it would serve the organization's building efforts to have top leaders step up and host these conferences on a weekly, if not more frequent, basis. Often, scheduling an opportunity call early in the week that feeds new distributors into a "get started training call" a couple of days later works well. Some keys to such a system's success include:

- Communicating the importance to support the calls. Calls that are poorly attended communicate the wrong impression to new listeners that this company must not be growing!
- The calls need to be high energy and interactive. It often works best when at least two leaders partner to co-lead the call, bouncing thoughts off each other.
- To conduct a powerful opportunity call, the presenter could first share her personal story regarding when and how she was introduced to the company, products, and opportunity. Where her life was before her involvement with her network marketing company can be contrasted with where she is now in terms of happiness, fulfillment, fun, and finances. She can briefly speak about the vehicle to create wealth, namely (1) network marketing, (2) the stability and credibility of the company, (3) the unique

qualities and value of the products, and (4) the exciting nature of the income opportunity. She can then ask for some product testimonials and then request some income testimonials.

Those distributors who share their stories and testimonials should stress the life-changing nature of the opportunity.

The call leader should thank all attendees, acknowledging those who generously shared their stories or offered testimonials.

Lastly, the call should end with a call to action, encouraging prospects to get with the person who invited them to the call to further explore the possibilities and have all their questions answered.

- Training calls should follow along with the company's duplicable system. For those companies that do not have such a definitive outline presenting exactly what to do to get started, I suggest using the 7-Step Success System as a guide. Initially, the training calls should focus on establishing the new distributors' reasons for joining and educating them on the network marketing concept.

Subsequent calls might include a brief summary of the company's compensation plan: (1) going over each of the products in detail to outline their benefits and target markets, (2) setting up the new distributor's office, (3) designing an action plan, (4) creating a names list and supplementary lead sources, and (5) role-playing some typical prospecting conversations.

The training call should stress the simplicity of the system. Using a prerecorded call to three-way in a prospect, offering a web site URL to visit, and suggesting a follow-up call with a success-line business partner are simple ways for even the most reluctant new team member to get started.

Local, Regional, and National Meetings

Your organization will grow most rapidly when you are able to take advantage of a strategy to funnel your prospects and distributors into local, regional, and national meetings. All company-approved meetings are promoted on all conference calls, in the monthly newsletter and bonus check flyers, on the corporate web site, and in all other communications to the field. Randy Anderson has built a dynasty utilizing this process of continually promoting the next impending event. Randy recommends the following strategies to make this structure work:

- Encourage local weekly meetings in all areas where a leader can take responsibility for hosting them and growing their attendance numbers. These meetings may be small at first, consisting of a local business builder who steps into leadership to invite a few guests or new distributors. As the local group grows in number, each distributor takes responsibility for inviting at least one new person to every weekly meeting. When the size of any particular weekly meeting reaches 15 or more, the group is encouraged to form a second local weekly gathering.

    As long as distributors continue to bring prospects and new distributors to these functions, the agenda can consist of a brief 30-minute opportunity introduction to the company, products, and income opportunity followed by a training focusing on some basic element of getting started properly to build a successful business.

    The entire weekly meeting should take no longer than two hours. It should be held on the same day and time and at the same place each week so as to avoid confusion. These meetings are best conducted in the comfortable confines of a home or office.

- The weekly meetings feed into the local monthly meetings. When these meetings are attended by at least 40 to 50 people, they can be hosted in a hotel or function facility meeting room. If they are smaller in size than that, it is best to conduct them in a home, office, or private restaurant room. It is important not to convey the impression that the business is not growing by holding poorly attended meetings in a formal, large meeting facility. The monthly meetings can start off with a brief opportunity presentation to support any prospects in attendance. All local leaders should share the room setup, agenda outline, and speaking assignments so as to edify everyone who has opted to step into a leadership role. The meeting should last between four and six hours and include lunch or dinner to add an element of fun and strengthen the relationships among attendees.
- The local monthly meetings serve to funnel people into larger regional meetings. These meetings typically are conducted in a hotel function facility. They last an entire day and end with a social and dinner event.

  It is valuable for a top distributor or accomplished leader to close these events. The ability to come and listen to someone who is living the dream, thanks to the great opportunity made possible by your company, is an important factor in stimulating interest and driving attendance.

  These meetings should focus on the steps to achieve success, with a goal of inspiring attendees to step into a massive action mode. They should also highlight success stories and recognize the accomplishment of distributors advancing in compensation plan positional rank and achieving organizational growth.

  Distributors should leave these functions motivated to share in the success they witnessed others already realizing.

They should also be inspired to commit to attending the company's national functions.

■ The national meetings are typically company supported and organized, though they may be conducted and head-lined by top field leaders. These meetings are often held in fun family resort locations, giving the distributor's family a reason to join him or her and make the event a memorable vacation.

Because these meetings have the goals of conducting trainings to equip distributors with important success distinctions, acknowledge leaders achieving success, introduce new products and programs, and most importantly to build relationships, partnerships and belief, it is best if meetings span the course of two or three days.

The intention of these events is to leave distributors with the knowledge of how to build a successful organization while inspiring their desire to go out and do whatever it takes to make this dream a reality. The most successful field leaders typically partner with the company's corporate team to make these events most powerful.

By creating such a structure with meetings at each level that feed other meetings, distributors are given the knowledge needed to build a successful business as well as a system to eventually transform new distributors into accomplished leaders. At each level, distributors are encouraged to stretch and step into a succession of leadership roles. Having such a structure also generates the excitement that comes from promoting the next impending event.

Prospect, Enroll, Train, and Do It All Again

It is important to stress the extreme value of combining training with massive action. Doing so will avoid your new partner's thinking that she will need to know every aspect of your product line and business plan before she can step into action. The most successful training lessons result from feedback that you will offer your new partner as she prospects and brings new people to the team. Be sure to let your new partners know that they have your full permission to mess up and fall flat on their faces. In fact, this is the most effective way for them to learn as they gather the successful distinctions that come with building a business. Many new distributors will be reluctant to make a mistake, thinking that they might blow a chance to enroll a great prospect. To the contrary, there is no scarcity of prospects in the world. Competence and eventual mastery will result from trial and error and never-ending improvement as part of the learning process.

By giving your team members plenty of room to make mistakes, you'll be encouraging them to step into their personal power. This power is greatly enhanced by your nonattachment to anyone needing to get involved. The posture you'll want to communicate is that you'd love any particular person to join your team—but the choice is theirs. You'll do quite well either way. There's no desperation and no scarcity of interested people who would welcome the chance to work with you in partnership toward their success. This logically takes us to the topic of personal improvement.

Step 6: PERSONAL DEVELOPMENT— GROW AS FAST AS YOUR ORGANIZATION DOES: CREATE STRUCTURES FOR PERSONAL EXCELLENCE

When you change the way you look at things,
the things you look at change.

—Anonymous

You may recall that we credited massive action as half of the equation essential for success. Well, the other half concerns how attractive you are as a sponsor and business partner and how effectively you are able to communicate your ability to support your prospects to realize their dreams. This chapter focuses upon how to create structures that will support your personal development and effectiveness.

IDENTIFY SOME AREAS TO WORK ON

Even the most experienced and seasoned network marketers can benefit from a program that examines their personal strengths and weaknesses.

Create a Personal Development Structure for Supporting Your Success

You're in consistent and persistent massive prospecting action. You are honoring your commitment to speak with a minimum number of prospects daily while following up with all interested parties on a timely basis. Let's look at some personal development structures you might put into place to gather feedback regarding how you can maximize your personal effectiveness with everyone you speak.

1. *Rate each prospecting communication you have* (1 = ineffective, self-absorbed, no rapport developed to 10 = powerful, rich value created, you've bonded with your prospect) *with respect to how powerfully you guided the conversation.*

Making Your Conversations Flow Most Effectively

Recall the five steps we discussed to ensure that your prospecting conversations are most effective:

Step 1: Create an opening to be heard.

Step 2: Determine if your prospect is open to exploring if there may be a fit with what you do by getting permission to ask him a few questions. Do this before discussing your income opportunity with him.

Step 3: Speak your commitment to your prospect in some way.

Step 4: Create rich possibilities that inspire action.

Step 5: End by making a request that moves the conversation in a forward direction.

After each conversation you have, review each of the five steps to analyze how effectively you accomplished each point. Ask yourself, "What worked about my conversation and what was missing, which if put into place would support my next conversation to be more productive and powerful?"

Start your analysis by focusing first upon *Step 1.* How well did you create an opening with your prospect? Did you develop sufficient rapport and discover what was

---

Making Your Conversations Flow *(Continued)*

important to her or missing in her life? Did you uncover the seeds of discontent to which your opportunity might contribute? How could you have been more effective in breaking the ice and creating an opening for your prospect to want to explore your offering without feeling pressure or obligation?

Work on the elements you perceive to be missing so that your next conversation is more productive. Once you've developed a degree of proficiency with this step, go on to *Step 2*. Ask yourself, "Did I get my prospect's permission to ask questions to explore how my opportunity may be a fit? Was I respectful of my prospect's time, or did I come across as pushy, arrogant, and intrusive? Did I dump information rather than ask questions to open up the conversation? Did I talk *at* this person, who had not yet agreed to look with me to explore a fit?"

Again, rate from 1 to 10 how well you accomplished these objectives and how you can do so more effectively next time. If you realize that you dumped information and did not fully explore what was important to your prospect, feel free to go back and refocus on these areas. Say something like, "Sally, I realized after we last spoke, I failed to ask you sufficiently about your goals and dreams. Let's assume that you agree to join our team in partnership and work with me toward your family's economic freedom. How much money would you need to be earning monthly a few years from now for you to be able to look back on this day as the day you made one of the best decisions of your life?" Once you determine how much residual income your prospect wants to earn, ask, "May I ask you one more question—when you're earning this amount of money each and every month, how would your life and the lives of

(Continues)

Making Your Conversations Flow *(Continued)*

your family be impacted? What would change? Would you buy a new home or car, travel more, work less, free yourself up to retire early, or put your kids through college?" You get the idea!

Don't step over your oversight. Go back and readdress it. Make a mental note to do so with your next prospect as well. Once you're satisfied with your progress in this area, work on *Step 3*.

Ask yourself, "Did I speak my commitment *first* to exploring a fit without obligation or pressure and *then* to my prospect's ultimate success? Does he know that I am on the path to success and if he chooses to join me, he can be as well? Does he know that I can show him exactly what it will take to reach the income level that will impact his life?" Similarly, with regard to *Step 4*, "Did I create such value that my prospect feels honored to have had me share my opportunity with him? Did I demonstrate to him, in simple terms, what it would take for him to be successful in this business? Did I effectively show him that he already knows several people who would be great in this business, and all he needs to do is set up a call for me to speak with them? Does he realize that he will not need to enroll a whole lot of people to be very successful in our company, just four to six business builders?" Again, rate yourself. Ask what's missing and commit to put these items in place for your next conversation.

Last, look to see if you made a powerful request to move the conversation in a forward direction that will support your prospect's needs and desires. Does she perceive your request as being in her best interest or self-serving to meet only *your* needs? Did you specify "by when" you are requesting that she take action and did she agree to your request? Have you set up a follow-up time to speak, so that you might support her to further learn about your company,

Making Your Conversations Flow *(Continued)*

products, and offering to see if they may be a fit for her life?

As you continue to analyze your effectiveness in each area, always ask yourself, "How could I create more value? How could I be more charismatic and effective in my communication? What's missing for me to have my skills reach the level of a masterful enroller?"

Though this self-discovery will yield many productive insights, there will always be areas where we are unable to see our own limitations. Without requesting the feedback of others who are skilled in listening for what may be missing in your communications, your conversations will likely reach a plateau in their efficacy. This brings us to our second personal development structure.

2. *Request that your sponsor or qualified business partner listen in on some of your calls or join you on some of your in-person presentations.* Better yet, listen to or sit in on several other successful enrollers' calls and meetings. Determine how they are able to move their conversations forward to achieve enrollment success. Pick up on important phrases, questions, and techniques that you might incorporate into your presentations. Alternate observing others with having them listen to you. Consider their feedback as possible places for you to look to improve upon your own presentations.

3. *Record several prospecting conversations.* You can purchase an inexpensive telephone-recording device and cassette recorder that can be used to create these tapes. Make a few copies of each tape and ask three of your coaches or success-line partners to listen to them at a time when they can take detailed notes to analyze what worked about each conversation and what was lacking to have it come across as most powerful and productive.

(Continues)

Making Your Conversations Flow *(Continued)*

4. *Ask your prospects for feedback.* Say something like, "John, I appreciate your speaking with me today and listening to some information about our company, product line, and income opportunity. I'm working on my listening and communication skills. Would you mind giving me some feedback with respect to a few areas? I would greatly appreciate your candid opinion." If your prospect agrees, ask, "Did you feel I was respectful of your time and opinions? Did you feel that I was interested in looking to see if our opportunity might contribute to your life, without pressure or obligation? Did you clearly understand how you could become successful in our business? Did you think that I created rich value or was something lacking in that regard? Would you like to share any insights you may have about how I could be more effective in future conversations?"

Thank your prospect for her contribution. If she is glad to support your growth, you might take advantage of her generosity by asking if she knows anyone who may be interested in earning an extra income.

5. *Hire a coach.* If you were a gifted athlete intent on qualifying to compete in the Olympic Games, you wouldn't consider *not* having a coach to champion your success. Why would striving to achieve great success in your business and your life be any different? A coach is a person who is trained to ask the right questions to get you to identify missing elements in these arenas. When these missing pieces are put in place, the result is a significant difference in your productivity, happiness, fulfillment, and your ability to impact others. Coaches go way beyond training. Training is about conveying information. Coaching is about gaining access to areas we are otherwise blind to discovering about our businesses and ourselves. Coaches cause breakthrough revelations by supporting us to explore the arena of what we don't know that we don't know. They champion our

Making Your Conversations Flow *(Continued)*

successes, our happiness, and our visions. Skilled coaches claim our goals as their own and act as our partners to look with us to see what's working optimally and what's missing that causes the results we are after to remain elusive. They listen to both what we say as well as to what is left unsaid. They do this by asking questions, exploring possibilities, making requests, and, at times, confronting issues that may need to be examined.

The most effective coaches are familiar with and skilled in the arenas in which they offer coaching support. In network marketing, no matter how skilled a coach may be, if she has not built a successful organization herself, there are likely many success distinctions that she may be missing in this arena to properly guide your success and accomplishment. An ideal network marketing coach will have the ability to train in successful methodology when needed. He will be well-versed in the art of how to maximize personal effectiveness, since so much about enrollment success depends upon how well we are able to listen to what's important to our prospects or missing in their lives and then to powerfully communicate the value inherent in our income opportunity.

For a coaching relationship to be most effective, you must be willing to look with your coach at whatever areas he suggests without becoming defensive or argumentative. Coaches typically do not have the answers themselves. Those being coached do. It is by knowing which questions to ask that coaches are able to best support their clients in examining areas that conceal breakthroughs in their understanding. Coaches bring out the best in others.

Coaching in the personal development arena can offer access to unleashing personal power and effectiveness. Of

(Continues)

Making Your Conversations Flow *(Continued)*

course, total confidentiality must exist to create the safety necessary to be able to explore any topic without fear of judgment or reprisals. Personal development coaching might involve such areas as impacting business productivity, enhancing relationships, achieving optimum health, creating wealth, or developing structures to champion personal effectiveness. True coaches are values-based and interact with those coached from a position of respect. At the same time, they operate from a commitment to rigor if that is what's needed to support someone to move forward. Effective coaches are committed to excellence and do not step over issues because of a desire to be liked or to avoid uncomfortable topics. They see their clients as totally capable of achieving breakthough success in any arena by listening for what may be missing, that if put into place, would fully honor the person's goals and values.

Many network marketing companies are blessed with competent coaches. Many also support personal development programs to champion their distributors to be their very best. If you'd like to explore a program to champion your productivity, success, and happiness, our company, the Center for Personal Reinvention, offers custom-tailored programs for individuals and groups. Read more about how we might support your life and business to work optimally at www.CenterForPersonalReinvention.com or contact me personally at DrJRubino@email.com.

Another suggestion would be to take on a self-study personal-development program. I wrote *The Power to Succeed:*

30 Principles for Maximizing Your Personal Effectiveness and *The Power to Succeed: More Principles for Powerful Living, Book II* for this very reason. You will find some excerpts at the web site just listed.

Grow Yourself along with Your Business

Using the following list as a memory jogger, identify the top five qualities of a successful leader and business partner *that would most impact your success.*

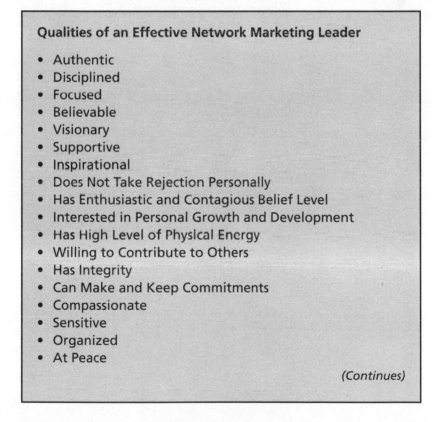

Qualities of an Effective Network Marketing Leader

- Authentic
- Disciplined
- Focused
- Believable
- Visionary
- Supportive
- Inspirational
- Does Not Take Rejection Personally
- Has Enthusiastic and Contagious Belief Level
- Interested in Personal Growth and Development
- Has High Level of Physical Energy
- Willing to Contribute to Others
- Has Integrity
- Can Make and Keep Commitments
- Compassionate
- Sensitive
- Organized
- At Peace

(Continues)

Network Marketing Leader Qualities *(Continued)*

- Persistent
- Consistent
- Teachable
- Empowers Others
- Ambitious
- Committed
- Entrepreneurial
- Team Player
- Confident
- Powerful
- Vulnerable
- Willing to Sacrifice for the Future
- Able to Bond with Others
- Positive, Upbeat Attitude
- Burning Desire to Succeed
- Follows Up and Follows Through
- Positive Expectation
- Works in Partnership
- Interested in Others
- Doesn't Dump Information
- Proactive—Takes Initiative
- Good Communication Skills
- Positive Expectation
- Committed
- Good Self-Image
- Intuitive
- Empathetic
- Happy to Serve
- Genuinely Humble
- Good Listener

In reinventing yourself to maximize your effectiveness, what qualities will support your declaration as a leader? Ask your coaches and partners for feedback about what qualities they see would best support your effectiveness and productivity in each area.*

Let's take a few moments to briefly define and discuss each quality or area in order to provide you with better insight regarding how each might apply to enhancing your productivity.

Authenticity is about how you come across to others. When what you say is in alignment with what you do and who you are, others perceive you as authentic. Authenticity comes from speaking in a conversational tone with an intention to communicate from your heart to the other person's heart. Contrast this with the opposite qualities of phoniness, hype, or falseness. Are you looking with your prospects to determine if your offering may be a fit or are you trying to sell him something he has no interest in considering? Might you resemble a sleazy salesperson trying to unload a broken-down, used car on a reluctant victim? *Believability* results from authentic communication and actions that display integrity. People who are believable avoid hype and exaggeration. They tell the truth responsibly, even when it becomes uncomfortable to do so. They follow through on the commitments they make and value their reputation over the convenience of saying or doing what's expedient at the moment.

---

*Adapted from *Secrets of Building a Million Dollar Network Marketing Organization from a Guy Who's Been There, Done That and Shows You How You Can Do It, Too* by Dr. Joe Rubino.

Discipline is about treating your income opportunity as a serious business. If you find yourself often watching television or making excuses to get out of prospecting, you lack this trait. The best example of a disciplined business builder is one who consistently honors her daily action commitment—no matter what the distractions and circumstances. On those days when it is impossible to do so, she commits to making up for the lapse with additional calls. People with discipline choose to honor their commitments to their vision rather than to their comfort and convenience.

Focus implies keeping your eye on the prize. It means ignoring distractions and effectively handling interruptions so they do not interfere with your achievements. During a conversation, focus is necessary to effectively guide a prospect by asking appropriate questions to support him in properly evaluating your offering. Having focus means returning yourself and your prospect to the topic at hand when it is obvious that you've strayed.

Visionaries see the big picture. They are not derailed by what they see as temporary challenges or interruptions en route to realizing their dreams. They inspire themselves and others to go after those things worth pursuing. They lead others to see possibilities in every situation rather than the limitations. They live out of a current, invigorating vision that empowers people by speaking what they are committed to achieving while challenging them to join in the quest.

Supportive leaders are team players. They create win-win scenarios wherever they go. They build relationships, empower others, and are champions of people and causes. In contrast, nonsupportive people are self-absorbed, with little interest in putting themselves in the other person's world. They fail to realize what their obstinacy is costing them in terms of generating possibilities and building relationships.

Inspirational people support others to see possibilities outside the box of usual familiarity. They are possibility thinkers, seeing ways to make things work where others do not. They are card-carrying visionaries who inspire others to join them in their visions and to create visions of their own.

Confident networkers know the value that their products and opportunity embody. They exude an attractiveness that causes others to want to join them and be in their presence. Confidence is born of *belief* in the gift they have to offer others. They share this gift with pride and positive expectation. Because of their confidence, they are self-motivated to stay in action, knowing for certain that their success is imminent.

Personal power results when one lives and acts in alignment with one's values. It, too, is a result of the confidence that comes from knowing one has the ability to impact the lives of others. People possessing personal power are charismatic and able to champion others to believe in themselves and achieve the type of success that results when actions are in alignment with vision. They are *proactive and take initiative* instead of waiting for things to fall into place by themselves. They realize there will always be challenges that allow those with a lesser commitment to make excuses and wait until the timing is just right to act. By taking *responsibility* for everything that shows up in their lives and in their businesses, these leaders realize that "if it's going to be, it's up to me!" They realize they are the source of whatever manifests around them and so they take it upon themselves to bring about the result they desire through *bold actions*.

Vulnerability does not imply weakness or failure. On the contrary, it's the ability to transparently convey who one really is on a personal or spiritual level. Vulnerability is the result of speaking and acting authentically. There is no need to hide, cover up, or pretend by wearing a mask. Others get who you really are because your actions are transparent. The most effective leaders possess a genuine humility that allows others to be comfortable in their presence. The opposites of vulnerability are callousness, arrogance, and defensiveness. One effective way to let others in and express vulnerability is to tell something about yourself that shows your humanity. Perhaps you might relay a story or share an incident that supports others to see the softer side you may ordinarily conceal from view. Ironically, many times, those individuals unafraid to share their vulnerability are perceived as inspirational and stronger because they do not hide their flaws. They, instead, use them to make others feel comfortable around them.

A *willingness to sacrifice for the future* is a quality essential to building a successful networking business. There will be many times when moving one's business forward will require a concerted effort in the present, regardless of whatever distractions may show up in life. Though it is wise to integrate life and business whenever possible, leaders, at times, will need to give their business priority over other distractions.

The ability to bond with others is a prerequisite for developing effective relationships and partnerships. Lone rangers do not make dynasty builders! There is simply no way to build a large, successful organization without empowering others to step into a leadership role. Empowerment comes from relationship-building and inspiring others to be their best. Supporting others to get to know you, like you, and trust you will strengthen the bonds that make for long-lasting relationships and business partnerships.

Leaders do not take rejection personally. They know that when prospects are not receptive to becoming involved in their opportunity, it has nothing to do with personal rejection. Perhaps the timing is not right for the prospect or they may not see themselves being successful in building a network marketing business. By not taking rejection personally, these leaders adopt an empowering interpretation that keeps them inspired to stay in massive action until such time as they identify enough other empowered, self-motivated leaders required to build their networking dynasty.

An enthusiastic and contagious belief level is the fire that spreads from those possessing this quality to those they prospect and those who join their team. Possessing this uplifting and charismatic *positive expectation* results from a surety that one is now, or soon will be, successful and so will those who join this person's organization. True belief comes across as an appealing and electrifying energy. It goes well beyond words alone to convey the genuine excitement that results from a certainty of achieving success. Those who are able to communicate this level of belief in the brightest possible future attract others with a magnetism that is lacking in those plagued by doubt and reservations.

An interest in personal growth and development separates those who make small, incremental advances from those who experience breakthrough performance levels. Those who commit to the process of constant and never-ending improvement in their lives and businesses are never content to stop learning and growing. They know that there is no arriving. The minute they forget this fact, they are back in the downward spiral that will kill their forward progress, damage their relationships, and remind them of their need to return to their commitment to perpetual growth and discovery. This quality separates the know-it-alls from those who view life as a continual process of self-discovery.

A *high level of physical energy and a positive, upbeat attitude* is important both from the standpoint of being able to sustain a busy schedule of prospecting, following up, training, and coaching as well as from the perspective of giving off an energy that is attractive to others. No one wants to partner with a person who appears ready to nod off to sleep at any minute. It is too easy to mistake low physical energy for lack of enthusiasm for what you do. An attractive energy level is upbeat but not frenetic. If you fear that your energy level may not be attractive to others, request feedback from your partners as you work on projecting a solid, empowering, and enthusiastic energy to everyone with whom you communicate.

A *willingness to contribute to others and work in partnership* is another attractive quality that will cause prospects to want to join us in partnership. People can smell a self-centered, me-first attitude a mile away. True leaders are *happy to serve* others. When our focus is on the success of others, we will be rewarded for our generosity of spirit tenfold. Prospects will clearly see our commitment to do whatever it takes to champion their success and will want to take advantage of this gift. The opposite quality of "what have you done for me lately?" communicated in what we say and don't say will repel others, who will seek to distance themselves from such a selfish and self-serving attitude. Because success in network marketing demands a commitment to working effectively in partnership, those who shun this trait find themselves without support, making their task that much more difficult. As a result of a commitment to be a *team player*, we will be much more likely to attract other team players who model our example.

Having integrity and the ability to make and keep commitments are important prerequisites for building trust. Integrity is simply walking your talk. People with integrity can be counted on by others to come through on their promises. Those lacking integrity will not be held in high esteem as leaders. Their word will be questioned and their ability to do what they say they will do will be doubted. After displaying a regular pattern of failing to follow through on commitments, one loses credibility as others decide to stay away to avoid letdown.

Compassion is the result of getting into the other person's shoes and experiencing his challenges as if they were your own. People appreciate those who have compassion for their situations. *Empathy* or an appreciation for what another is going through is not the same as sympathy, which implies feeling bad for another whom we hold as incapable of dealing with the adversity presented. We can have compassion for the challenges of others without buying into their excuses or lack of commitment.

Possessing sensitivity allows us to be aware of the difficulties inherent in a situation. Those lacking sensitivity are wrapped up in their own world, often at the expense of others. This negative quality repels others who see insensitive people as cold, aloof, or unfeeling. Others will be more likely to want to work in partnership with those who possess the sensitivity of appreciating the challenges and limitations of others.

Organized people are typically productive people. Those lacking organizational skills frequently drop the ball and let others down because they are unable to effectively manage and honor their commitments. Organizational skills are necessary to make the most effective use of time. Often, those lacking these skills simply require a support structure to assist them in their ability to lend order to their lives and businesses. Such structures may include adding a PalmPilot, day planner, contact software, filing system, or other reminder or organizational system to set priorities and add a degree of order to replace chaos. Becoming organized means gaining clarity about your priorities and taking responsibility for recording them, classifying them, and honoring them.

Being at peace conveys energy conducive to having others want to be around you. On the contrary, nervousness, worry, fear, sadness, and anger repel others. Leaders who project this positive and attractive energy possess a *positive self-image*. Their high self-esteem supports them in *handling rejection* and *not taking things personally* while *attributing positive interpretations* to things that people say and do that allow them to remain upbeat and empowered rather than reactive and easily discouraged. Those who are at peace know that there are always valuable lessons to be learned at all times and with all matters. By trusting that things work out for the best and knowing that there is wisdom behind all worldly happenings, it serves us to trust that we will be fine in the end and can go about our days with the peace and serenity that come from this knowledge.

Consistency in network marketing refers to regularly repeated actions that will support a desired result. The best example of a consistent action plan is a *daily action commitment*, namely a pledge to engage in a minimum number of conversations on a daily basis. *Persistency* implies tenacious follow-up. It is such a commitment to *follow-up and follow through* that will produce the greatest returns. Consistency (daily new prospecting conversations) without persistency (following up until obtaining a yes, no, or try me later—or at least six attempts to connect with a prospect)—will not produce the maximum number of enrollments possible. You will find that some of your most productive leaders will result from the persistency of a fourth, fifth, or sixth contact attempt.

Being teachable and coachable is a necessary element of duplication, and duplication is necessary for the maximum growth of an organization. Teachable team members are open to learning about and implementing processes that work. Coachability refers to an openness to listen to and consider feedback to explore ways to be more effective with people and more productive in growing the business. I invite people resistant to being trained or coached to give it their best shot in their own way and when they are ready to take on a proven system that works to let me know. In the meantime, I will make myself available to speak with any of their prospects via a three-way call. It is only when they decide to follow a proven methodology that I will work closely in a coaching relationship with them.

Being interested in others and aware of the need to empower them is an essential component for building leaders. We must be sincerely interested in their well-being, while willing to commit to *their* success, not just our own. When we seek to manipulate or control others, we make them small and dependent upon us for their confidence and power. Since our income in network marketing is usually proportional to the number of leaders we empower to step into a leadership role of their own, failure to make others great will dramatically impact our bottom line.

An ambitious and burning desire to succeed together with an *entrepreneurial nature* will support people to do whatever is necessary to build a huge networking business. However, be aware that desire alone without a *positive expectation* to succeed will not be sufficient to manifest success. Desire alone represents the wanting of something that is currently missing or not yet attained. Look at how many people *want* to be rich and happy but are poor and miserable, instead! Consider how many overweight people *want* to be thin. Wanting or desiring alone, without a positive expectation focuses on the absence of what is desired rather than on the belief in its ultimate manifestation. So to be most empowering, combine a burning desire with an unshakable belief in the end result you seek.

Commitment to achieving a result is certainly one of the most critical qualities essential for success in network marketing. We are all committed to something. But that something is often our comfort or convenience, rather than doing whatever it takes to generate a desired result. I like to picture myself standing at a fork in the road. On the left-hand path lies the path of least resistance, the easy way out. It often represents the choices of looking good or of being liked over saying what needs to be said in a responsible manner to ensure we are heard. It may mean doing what we feel like doing instead of honoring our commitment to our vision and to staying in massive action. It may mean lying or stepping over the truth instead of doing the right thing and speaking our truth responsibly. In contrast, the right-hand path represents the path of heart, the road to our dreams' fulfillment. Moment by moment, we have the ability to recognize our chance to choose and decide deliberately to follow the path that will support our goals and vision, instead of our comfort. As a key part of your personal development plan, pay attention to the many opportunities you have daily to select the path of heart rather than the path of convenience. You will successfully develop this skill by continually recognizing your ability to choose and then acting in alignment with your commitments.

Being a good listener with good communication skills is critical to leaving our prospects with a sense that they have been heard and honored. Being a good listener means both asking insightful questions and then quietly listening to what the person has to say without interrupting. Successful networkers listen to what others say, and, just as importantly, listen to what they do not say. They are highly *intuitive*. Often, by reading between the lines and paying attention to the unspoken communication, we can derive our greatest insights into where our prospects are in the discussion. We are always listening to something. However, too often that something is the frenetic chatter going on in our own brains, instead of what our prospects are really saying. To be a good listener, all it takes is to recognize when you are not listening and simply to return yourself to your commitment to listen attentively. Good listeners *do not simply dump information* upon their prospects. They do not talk at others but speak to them, ever mindful of not cutting them off or of stepping over their concerns, questions, and statements.*

*For an in-depth discussion of the art of listening, see *The Power to Succeed: 30 Principles for Maximizing Your Personal Effectiveness* and *The Power to Succeed: More Principles for Powerful Living, Book II* by Dr. Joe Rubino.

To create your own personal development structure to support your business success, start by selecting your top 5 to 10 areas upon which to focus. Use the same structures we previously discussed to gauge your improvement on a daily basis. Decide to work on one quality at a time, starting with those traits you believe would make the greatest impact on your business if you were to master them. After each conversation you have, rate yourself with respect to how well you manifested that particular quality. Ask yourself, "How can I enhance my next conversation by addressing this area?" Look also at those skills where you are not yet proficient. Declare yourself a novice in these areas and decide to work toward the goal of eventually developing mastery in each area. Always ask yourself, "What may be missing, that if put into place, would enhance this trait or area of development?" Success in taking on the positive traits you discover to be missing is as simple as recognizing when the particular qualities are absent and taking bold action to focus on putting them into place.

Personal Development Means Having the Ability to Generate Positive Interpretations on an Ongoing Basis

Success in network marketing is often due to how well we respond to the rejection and other daily challenges that assault our belief level and threaten to throw us off track. It's rarely the actual words or situation that throws us into a tailspin. Rather, it's how we react to these words and events. The way in which we interpret another's statements and the meanings we attribute to those problematic situations present for us the real challenge. If you find yourself too often at the mercy of your negative emotions, that is, being angry, sad, or afraid, please pay close attention to this section! Your ability to be seven-feet tall and bulletproof in dealing with whatever problems may arise is often a function of how well you execute the 3 R's: *Recognize, Release,* and *Reinterpret.*

Recognize!   The key to maximizing your personal power often begins with your ability to recognize the opportunity to stop for a moment, evaluate your possible responses to any situation, and then act in a manner that reflects your personal power and effectiveness. This is often different from the way you would usually respond to such an occurrence in the heat of the moment. Your power begins by first recognizing your ability to *not react* to a stimulus but instead to deliberately respond in a manner that supports you. Reacting usually is the sort of behavior consistent with a mood of anger, fear, or sadness. The mood is your red flag to stop and to recognize that you now have an opportunity to step into your power. According to Mike Smith of Bridgequest, anger is most people's predominant mood. If this is true for you, you will be well served to recognize when your anger flares up! It will be your cue to take the next step, which is to *release* the emotion. If you are one of those individuals who go quickly to the emotion of fear, recognizing this emotional flag will give you a warning sign to catch yourself in the act of being afraid. Similarly, if your predominant emotional reaction to stressful events is sadness, this emotion will signal your opportunity to choose your next actions wisely.

Release!   Once you've identified your opportunity to notice your reactive emotion of anger, fear, or sadness, you can decide to deliberately release this emotion and the accompanying interpretation that has brought it about. Again, it's usually not the exact words that someone says or the action that takes place that brings about your anger, sadness, or fear. It's instead the meaning that you attribute to these words or actions. You make up interpretations that make you angry, sad, or afraid.

For example, in speaking with your prospect, he may say, "Is this one of those pyramid schemes?" For some, this question will evoke anger. You may think, "How dare he accuse me of being involved with an illegal, sleazy pyramid scheme!" For others, it may generate fear. You may think, "Does he know something I do not? Can I get into trouble?" For others still, this question might bring about the emotion of sadness. "Here's yet another person who's finding a reason to reject me!"

Let's analyze what happened a bit closer. Mr. Prospect simply asked a question. Perhaps he was involved in a pyramid scheme at one time and lost money or got into trouble with the law. Perhaps he was testing our knowledge of our opportunity. Maybe he was looking for a way to make some fast money and was excited about this possibility. Maybe he was afraid you were going to ask him to spend money, and he was looking for an excuse to give him a way out. You simply do not know his motivation. So do not make something up that causes you to be angry, sad, or afraid! Release the mood you feel coming on along with the interpretation you created that resulted in the generation of your mood.

Reinterpret.   Since we can't possibly know exactly what your prospect meant by his question, let's give him the benefit of the doubt and reinterpret it in such a way that allows us to further explore it, while remaining mood-free. We might take the interpretation that the prospect is interested in getting involved and is simply asking questions to establish the company's legitimacy. We might further interpret that he is providing us with an opportunity to listen to his concern and to educate him about the sterling reputation of your company and opportunity. We might see his question as a legitimate fear that he wants to resolve so he can move forward to the next level. Since we do not know what it's like in his world, we can't possibly know the true source of his question. So let's reinterpret it in a way that allows us to retain our power by gaining clarity about what his inquiry is all about. We might define his objection and say something like, "Tell me a bit more about your concern. Have you had a bad experience before with a pyramid scheme?" Or we might embellish his objection and say, "That's a great question! I also was concerned about the legitimacy of the opportunity when it was first presented to me. After all, there really are so many sleazy schemes out there! The last thing I'd want to get involved with is a company that is lacking integrity even the slightest bit." By not reacting emotionally, you can now maximize your ability to address your prospect's concern without the baggage of responding from a state of anger, fear, or sadness.

You will have ample opportunities in your network marketing business and in your daily life to recognize the opportunity to release an emotion that does not serve your personal power. Reinterpret your situation in such a way that you are personally empowered to respond in a manner that best serves your happiness, productivity, and effectiveness in communication. As you go about your day, notice when you become angry, sad, or afraid. Separate the facts regarding what was said or done from what meaning you attributed to these words or deeds. Create a new interpretation that has no negative emotions attached to it. This new meaning will keep you in relationship with the other person by giving her the benefit of the doubt. Your commitment to recognize the opportunity to respond to situations without the emotional baggage that diminishes your personal power will support effective communication and success in your business and relationships.*

CONVERSATIONS FOR SUCCESS: A COURSE IN PERSONAL AND PRODUCTIVITY DEVELOPMENT

For those interested in a deeper personal development discussion, while breaking through all life and business challenges, the Center for Personal Reinvention offers a three-day program entitled *Conversations for Success: A Course in Personal and Productivity Development for Network Marketers and Others* that has been described by many as simply life-changing. To follow is a more detailed description of the program.

The world we live and work in is marked by unprecedented change and fraught with new and complex challenges. For many of us, our network marketing businesses and our lives begin to look like an uphill struggle to survive instead of a fun and exciting opportunity to grow, risk, and play full out in partnership with others. The stresses, conflicts, and frustrations we experience daily need not be so.

There exists another possibility:

To live and work in choice, empowered by the challenges of life

To champion others to achieve excellence in a nurturing environment that fosters partnerships

---

*For a more thorough discussion of how to effectively manage your moods and respond to challenges in a way that support your personal effectiveness, see *Restore Your Magnificence: A Life-changing Guide to Reclaiming Your Self-esteem* by Dr. Joe Rubino.

To acquire the success principles that support mutuality, creativity, and harmony

To take on the art of listening and communicating in such a way that others are impacted to see new possibilities for accomplishment, partnership, and excellence

Reinventing ourselves, our relationships, and our perceptions are the results of a never-ending commitment to our own personal magnificence and to that of others. It is made possible through the acquisition of approximately 50 key principles that cause people to begin to view life and people in an entirely different way. When people really *get* these principles, their lives, relationships, and new possibilities for breakthroughs show up from a totally fresh perspective. Through the use of cutting edge technology as a vibrant basis for learning, growing, and acting, the Center for Personal Reinvention is successful in shifting how life shows up for people by supporting them to self-discover these life-changing principles.

With this program, you will:

- Uncover the secrets to accessing your personal power while maximizing your business productivity.
- Gain clarity on exactly what it will take to reach your network marketing and life goals with velocity.
- Create a structure for enhancing your effectiveness with others while developing new and empowering partnerships.
- Learn how taking total responsibility for every aspect of your life and your network marketing business can result in breakthrough performance.
- Discover what the key elements are to a detailed action plan and how to reach your goals in record time.

- Acquire the keys to listening and communicating effectively and intentionally.
- Recognize and shift out of self-defeating thoughts and actions.
- Gain the insight to better understand others with new compassion and clarity.
- Learn how to develop the charisma necessary to attract others to you.
- Experience the confidence and inner peace that comes from stepping into leadership.

The Center for Personal Reinvention offers customized courses and programs personally designed for achieving maximum results. Areas of focus include:

Designing Your Future

Making Life and Businesses Work Optimally

Generating Infinite Possibilities

Creating Conversations for Mutuality

Commitment Management

Personal Coaching and Development

Maximizing Personal Effectiveness

Productivity Breakthrough

Leadership Development

Relationship and Team Building

Conflict Resolution

Listening for Solutions

Systems for Personal Empowerment

Personal and Productivity Transformation

Designing Structures for Accomplishment

Listening in New, Empowered Ways

Possibility Thinking

Methods of Effectively Moving Action Forward

Structures for Team Accountability

Innovative Thinking

Completing with The Past

Creating a Life of No Regrets

The Center for Personal Reinvention champions companies and individuals to achieve their potential through customized programs addressing specific needs consistent with their vision for the future. Contact us today to explore how we might impact your world!

The Center for Personal Reinvention
PO Box 217, Boxford, MA 01921
drjrubino@email.com
Tel.: (888) 821-3135
Fax: (630) 982-2134

Step 7: STEPPING INTO LEADERSHIP: THE KEYS TO DEVELOPING OTHER SELF-MOTIVATED LEADERS

*If I have seen farther than others,
it is because I was standing on the shoulder of giants.*
—Isaac Newton

Permit me to expound upon my story as it relates to the topic of leadership. As I've shared, when I was first introduced to network marketing, I was a full-time dentist operating my own successful practice. Although I was proficient at the art of dentistry and running a practice, I considered myself anything but a leader. My shyness was responsible for my self-imposed isolation. I hid within the walls of my office. I was so determined to protect myself from the discomfort of meeting new people and expanding my social circles by attending dental functions that I opted to satisfy my continuing education requirements by mail. Not only would I not consider myself a leader back then, but the truth is I made a pretty poor follower as well!

At the same time, I was intrigued by the possibility of creating a lifelong residual income to replace my six-figure dental income. To my dismay, I soon discovered that building the type of impressive network marketing dynasty necessary to generate the level of income I would need to transition out of dental practice required skills (and courage) that I knew were missing from the cozy, safe, and sheltered box I had constructed around my personal world. I came to the realization that I would need to reinvent myself and step into a leadership role in my newly chosen profession of network marketing if I had *any* chance of realizing my dreams.

With this commitment fueling my actions, I mustered the courage to enroll in a yearlong program to reinvent the person I had become over the previous 35 years. That program has since turned into a never-ending commitment to personal development for those I champion who desire to be their very best, as well as for me. I decided after that first year that I would commit my life to not only being a good follower and perpetual student but also to declare myself a leader in the arenas of personal development and network marketing. As a result of this decision, I was able to build a successful organization with a multimillion dollar asset-value by showing others how to do the same. My success began when I made the decision to step into leadership.

I share this story to stress the simple fact that if I could transform myself from being an introverted, deeply resigned dentist who "couldn't lead three people in silent prayer" to a successful author, speaker, trainer, and coach, anyone can transform who decides to adopt the same principles that supported my own reinvention.

Stepping into a leadership role always begins with a decision to do so. No matter what evidence we may have accumulated to convince ourselves to the contrary, we all possess the power to be transformed into self-declared, empowered leaders whenever we decide to take the leap. How do you take this leap? The same way you jump off a mountain. You just do it!

For a leader, the decision to lead is always followed by a declaration. We each possess the personal power to declare our new commitment to leadership. The decision to lead is never contingent upon our past. Most of us can prepare a pretty strong case backed by all sorts of disempowering evidence to support that we are *not* leaders. By boldly declaring our new commitment to lead, we now get to determine exactly what leadership will look like for us. We can take responsibility for formulating a clear and compelling vision of how our leadership will manifest into the world. We also get to envision the results of this leadership and the effect it will have on the lives of others and on the world at large.

Leadership means that we are committed to powerfully acting in alignment with our commitments and vision. (This is yet another reason for clarifying, reading daily, and frequently speaking the inspirational vision we crafted in Step #1.) Contrary to our cultural paradigm, leaders often do not have all the answers. Many times, they simply need to risk and act from their values, in line with the results they desire to manifest. As self-appointed leaders, we can ask ourselves, moment by moment, "What would a leader do in this situation?" By asking this question, we decide to act in a manner congruent with how we see ourselves—as leaders!

In our network marketing businesses, we can apply these principles to step into leadership whenever we choose. No evidence is required to support this decision. Our decision to lead is not based upon volume or company position. Our decision to step into leadership results simply from a courageous commitment to act as a leader on a continual basis.

THE ELEMENTS OF NETWORK MARKETING LEADERSHIP

As network marketing leaders, let's examine some components critical to effective leadership.

1. At the foundation of any decision to lead lies a clear and compelling vision. Your vision as a successful network marketing leader will encompass every aspect of your life and business. It will include a clear and motivating representation of the person you have decided to be. It will honor your most important values and reflect the manifestation of your life purpose as you share your unique gifts with the world. When you live your vision, your days will be spent in choice. As a result, you will manifest those things into reality that results from accomplishing the ideals most important to you. Your vision will serve to motivate you to overcome all challenges and to do what's necessary to achieve the success you desire. Powerful visions are most effective when spoken at every opportunity. By speaking your vision, you will inspire others to want to join you in its accomplishment. You will also inspire many to create visions of their own, moved by your example. Your life will become an example of how a positive expectation can empower others to achieve breakthrough results in their network marketing businesses and in their lives.

As a network marketing leader, you will become proficient in showing people how to think *outside the box* to manifest great possibilities in their lives. As you incorporate vision work into your basic training, you will be sharing a gift that has the ability to empower and transform lives marked by resignation and suffering. You will inspire others to pursue their dreams with a newfound hope and expectation of success. More importantly, by teaching others to teach others to design lives that work optimally, you'll be duplicating the gift of empowerment and contributing the tools that can form a successful foundation of accomplishment and leadership.

Leadership Exercise: Write out in vivid detail what your expectations for leadership in your business will look like.

2. Leaders execute bold action plans that move their lives and businesses in a forward manner. Visions without actions are not really visions after all; they are wishful hopes void of the power of commitment and positive expectation. Leaders take responsibility for manifesting their visions by formulating specific, detailed, and grounded action plans that will bring them about. They continually evaluate whether their actions are sufficient in quantity and effective enough in quality to make their visions come true. Network marketing leaders are well-served to evaluate the efficacy of their actions on a weekly basis and make the adjustments necessary to realize their goals. They know that in order to inspire others and generate a result, their actions must be consistent over time and persistent in frequency. Successful networking leaders know their enrollment ratios—how many prospects they will need to speak with, on average, in order to identify and develop an on-fire, do-whatever-it-takes leader. They execute a long-term action commitment to speak with a minimum number of prospects about their business every day so that, based upon their success-ratios, they will bring about the number of new leaders necessary to build a business dynasty.

> *Leadership Exercise:* What specific daily action commitment will you undertake for the next 90 days? What actions are necessary for you to experience a breakthrough in your business growth?

3. Leaders possess an unshakable belief in their ultimate success and in the success of those who join them in partnership to follow a grounded, detailed action plan. This belief comes across to others as infectious, enthusiastic, and inevitable. True leaders possess the ability to inspire this certainty of future accomplishment to their prospects and team members. They know and teach their partners that a positive expectation of success in building their network marketing dynasties will generate sufficient self-motivation to manifest this goal into reality. They also know that the opposite is also true: When one expects to fail, this expectation generates self-sabotage and resignation, eventually resulting in quitting and an interpretation of failure. Either way, belief produces a self-fulfilling prophecy. Because of this knowledge, by virtue of their actions, leaders instill belief in the network marketing concept, their company, products, income opportunity, and in their own leadership abilities and those of their partners.

> *Leadership Exercise*: Identify any areas where your own belief level is inconsistent with building a network marketing dynasty. Consult with your coaches to put any missing elements into place to solidify your expectation of success.

4. The most effective network marketing leaders display a transparent authenticity and attitude of service that endears them to those who partner with them. Leaders walk their talk by demonstrating that their actions are consistent with their promises. They build trust and credibility as they prove they can be counted upon by demonstrating their commitment time and again to the success of their partners. Effective network marketing leaders avoid hype, arrogance, and domination. They, instead, choose sincerity, genuine humility, and a commitment to champion and serve others. They know that projecting a false façade diminishes their personal effectiveness and ability to manifest their intended results on an organizational basis. They work on effectively listening to others, always looking for ways to better impact their ability to achieve success and realize their dreams.

Leadership Exercise: How does your own leadership style limit your personal effectiveness? What qualities will you seek to develop to enhance your ability to impact others?

5. Successful network marketing leaders duplicate themselves by empowering others to step into a leadership role at every opportunity. They make others great, never small through manipulation or condescension. They do this through making powerful requests that have others see new possibilities that they may not have previously seen for themselves, always stretching them to grow outside their comfort zones.

Effective leaders become proficient at the art of acknowledgment, always on the lookout to catch others doing something right. They realize that their own success depends upon their ability to champion up-and-coming partners to become even more effective and impactful leaders than they were. They know that there is no shortage of opportunities to build leadership. They are ever vigilant for ways to take a step aside, out of the limelight, in order to support another person to shine and gain recognition.

Leadership Exercise: Take on the art of empowering your leaders to greatness. Make at least one request and offer at least one sincere acknowledgment on a daily basis with this objective in mind.

Practical Steps to Taking On a Leadership Role

Now that you have declared yourself to be a network marketing leader, it's time to seek out every possible opportunity to stretch who you are and step into your leadership role. Here are a few ways you might begin.

1. Be the source of leadership events in your local area. Commit to holding regularly scheduled weekly meetings at your home or office. If you do not have a home or office environment that lends itself to professional meetings, schedule them in a quiet room in a coffee shop or restaurant. It's important that you hold the meetings regularly, no matter how poor the attendance at first. The fact that others will see you as the local leader, taking responsibility for making these meetings happen, will help to establish your local leadership role. In the beginning, you might be the only person prospecting in your area and inviting others to attend your weekly function. As word gets out about your weekly meetings, more and more people will eventually attend and the numbers will build. There will come a day when it will grow to the extent that your meeting will be best supported to break up into a second and then a third local meeting. This will provide you with an opportunity to champion your own leaders to claim their personal power and adopt this leadership role themselves.

2. Volunteer to speak in front of the room at your local monthly and regional meetings. Perhaps you will take on a particular product presentation or speak about some aspect of your company's compensation plan. You may start your public speaking career with a brief 5- to 15-minute segment on a topic you feel confident about addressing. Perhaps you might volunteer to be part of a panel, with each panel member speaking about a specific product or aspect of business building. This is a great way to learn to field audience questions in a format that allows support from others in case you require assistance with some of the more difficult questions. No mat-

ter what your confidence level, commit to taking baby steps to support your public speaking confidence and ability to entertain, educate, and impact a crowd. Become involved with your local Toastmasters organization to practice your public speaking skills on a friendly, supportive crowd. You might even interest a number of your fellow Toastmasters in your income opportunity!

3. Commit to host and lead a weekly opportunity or training call to introduce and support others in your growing organization or partner with other leaders cross-line by opening up the call to your entire company. By becoming the force for others to get together on a weekly call, you will be contributing to the growth of your own organization and those of others whom you will be inspiring with your leadership.

4. Set up an accountability circle with three or four other distributors. These can be leaders in your own organization or cross-line in your company. Commit to reporting your actions to the other members of this "hot team" daily via e-mail or weekly with a group conference call. Follow the following format in reporting your daily actions:

- What is your daily action commitment (number of prospecting, follow-up, and acceleration conversations)? A good starting point might be a daily commitment to 3/2/1, that is, three new prospecting conversations, two follow-up conversations, and one acceleration conversation to move a prospect or new distributor to the next level.
- Did you meet your commitment to have this many conversations? If not, how many people did you speak with?
- What worked about your conversations?
- What was missing, that if put into place, will make your next conversations more productive and effective?

EPILOGUE: TYING THE 7-STEPS TOGETHER TO BUILD YOUR NETWORK MARKETING DYNASTY

The 7-Steps outlined in this book can serve as your road map to building your very own network marketing dynasty. As we've discussed many times in this book, success in network marketing ultimately requires the development of empowered, self-motivated leaders who implement and utilize systems that allow duplication of their efforts in championing and supporting the success of others.

Success ultimately depends upon leadership, and leadership always begins with the crystallization of a powerful and inspirational vision. A vision that truly motivates and inspires its creator and the people he or she will impact demands a detailed, grounded, and regularly updated action plan to bring about its realization. For a new distributor, such a plan initially begins with a focus on prospecting, since speaking with others about the income opportunity is the only activity that will directly result in influencing a new organization's growth. Prospecting success is both the result of consistent and persistent massive action and creating value through effective communication. When you are confident about the worth of your company's income opportunity and effective at conveying this value, while being simultaneously aware of what is important to your prospect and how your offering might best impact her life, you will become masterfully proficient at enrollment.

Once you are effective at attracting others to partner with you, you'll want to train them to powerfully communicate to others the value they've seen. This will enable them to duplicate your efforts. The means to dramatically accelerating and enhancing one's personal power and communication skills is a personal development program that will support a leader's effectiveness and power. The ultimate goal of such a program will be to support each individual to assume a prominent leadership role in the organization and to take responsibility for duplicating this entire process over and over. The result is a dynamic team of mutually empowering and personally empowered individuals who are totally committed to the personal and financial freedom of others. By following a duplicable success system, such as the one presented in this book, as you champion your team to identify and develop other on-fire leaders committed to massive, effective action, you will discover the secrets to building an ever-expanding network marketing dynasty.

One last point to remember is in order here. Building a network marketing dynasty shares nothing in common with the many shady get rich quick schemes that serve only to tarnish the reputation of the worthy, legitimate companies and their long-lasting income opportunities. Mastery in any profession does not come overnight or without a proper appreciation for developing the many foundational principles that are essential to erect an organization characterized by sound business-building principles and deep, lasting, committed, and trusting relationships. Success in network marketing will result from the process of simultaneously learning, doing, and teaching as you go. There will never arrive a time when you have learned everything there is to know. There is no shortage of people out there waiting for you to open the golden door of opportunity for them, ready to fall in. For these reasons, I suggest you not delay in getting started on your path to building your dynasty, thinking, perhaps, that there is so much to learn before you can possibly be ready. Whether you are new to our great industry or if you have been involved as a distributor for years, decide today to declare yourself a leader, and begin to follow a duplicable system that will insure your success and the success of your partners and friends. Commit to becoming a perpetual student in the never-ending learning process of maximizing your personal effectiveness and ability to impact the lives of others. By all means, do not forget to have fun in the process as you share the potentially life-changing gift of network marketing with others. I wish you tremendous success on your quest.

Live long and sponsor!

—Joe Rubino

> No great thing is created suddenly, any more than
> a bunch of grapes or a fig. If you tell me that you
> desire a fig, I answer you that there must be time.
> Let it first blossom, then bear fruit, then ripen.
> —Epictetus

RECOMMENDED READINGS:
OTHER BOOKS BY DR. JOE RUBINO

The Power to Succeed:
30 Principles for Maximizing Your Personal Effectiveness

What exactly distinguishes those who are effective in their relationships, productive in business, and happy, powerful, and successful in their approach to life from those who struggle, suffer, and fail? That is the key question that *The Power to Succeed: 30 Principles for Maximizing Your Personal Effectiveness* explores in life-changing detail. The information, examples, experiences, and detailed exercises offered will produce life-altering insights for readers who examine who they *are being* on a moment-to-moment basis that either contributes to increasing their personal effectiveness, happiness and power—or not. As you commit to an inquiry around what it takes to access your personal power, you will gain the tools to overcome any challenges or limiting thoughts and behavior and will discover exactly what it means to be the best you can be.

With this book YOU will:

- Uncover the secrets to accessing your personal power.
- Create a structure for maximizing your effectiveness with others.
- Learn to take total responsibility for everything in your life.

- Discover the key elements to accomplishment and how to reach your goals in record time.
- Identify your life rules and discover how honoring your core values can help you maximize productivity.
- Complete your past and design your future on purpose.
- Discover the keys to communicating effectively and intentionally.
- Stop complaining and start doing.
- Seize your personal power and conquer resignation in your life.
- Learn how to generate conversations that uncover new possibilities.
- See how embracing problems can lead to positive breakthroughs in life.
- Leave others whole while realizing the power of telling the truth.
- Learn how to develop the charisma necessary to attract others to you.

The Power to Succeed: More Principles for Powerful Living, Book II

This revealing book continues where *The Power to Succeed: 30 Principles for Maximizing Your Personal Effectiveness* left off, with more powerful insights into what it takes to be most happy, successful, and effective with others.

With this book YOU will:

- Discover the keys to unlock the door to success and happiness.
- Learn how your listening determines what you attract to you.
- How to shift your listening to access your personal power.

- See how creating a clear intention can cause miracles to show up around you.
- Learn the secrets to making powerful requests to get what you want from others.
- Discover how to fully connect with and champion others to realize their greatness.
- Learn to create interpretations that support your excellence and avoid those that keep you small.
- Develop the power to speak and act from your commitments.
- See how communication with others can eliminate unwanted conditions from your life.
- Discover the secret to being happy and eliminating daily upsets.
- Learn how to put an end to gossip and stop giving away your power.
- Develop the ability to lead your life with direction and purpose and discover what it's costing you not to do so.
- And More!!

The Power to Succeed: 30 Principles for Maximizing Your Personal Effectiveness and its sequel, *The Power to Succeed: More Principles for Powerful Living, Book II* are a powerful course in becoming the person you wish to be. Read these books, take on the success principles discussed, and watch your life and business transform and flourish.

The Magic Lantern:
A Fable about Leadership, Personal Excellence and Empowerment

Set in the magical world of Center Earth, inhabited by dwarves, elves, goblins, and wizards, *The Magic Lantern* is a tale of personal development that teaches the keys to success and happiness. This fable examines what it means to take on true leadership while learning to become maximally effective with everyone we meet.

Renowned personal development trainer, coach, and veteran author, Dr. Joe Rubino tells the story of a group of dwarves and their young leader, who go off in search of the secrets to a life that works, a life filled with harmony and endless possibilities and void of the regrets and upsets that characterize most people's existence. With a mission to restore peace and harmony to their village in turmoil, the characters overcome the many challenges they encounter along their eventful journey. Through self-discovery, they develop the principles necessary to be the best that they can be as they step into leadership and lives of contribution to others.

The Magic Lantern teaches us:

- The power of forgiveness
- The meaning of responsibility and commitment
- What leadership is really all about
- The magic of belief and positive expectation
- The value of listening as an art
- The secret to mastering one's emotions and actions
- And much more

It combines the spellbinding storytelling reminiscent of Tolkien's *The Hobbit* with the personal development tools of the great masters.

The Legend of the Light-Bearers: A Fable about Personal Reinvention and Global Transformation

Is it ever too late for a person to take on personal reinvention and transform his or her life? Can our planet right itself and reverse centuries of struggle, hatred, and warfare? Are love, peace, and harmony achievable possibilities for the world's people? *The Legend of the Light-Bearers* is a tale about vision, courage, and commitment, set in the magical world of Center Earth. In this much anticipated prequel to Dr. Joe Rubino's internationally best-selling book, *The Magic Lantern: A Fable about Leadership, Personal Excellence and Empowerment*, the process of personal and global transformation is explored within the guise of an enchanting fable. As the action unfolds in the world following the great Earth Changes, this personal development parable explores the nature of hatred and resignation, the secrets to transformation, and the power of anger and the means to overcoming it and replacing it with love. It shows what can happen when people live values-based lives and are guided by their life purposes instead of their destructive moods and their need to dominate others. If ever our world needed a road map to peace and cooperation and our people, a guide to personal empowerment and happiness, they do now . . . and this is the book.

Secrets of Building a Million Dollar Network Marketing Organization from a Guy Who's Been There, Done That and Shows You How You Can Do It, Too.

Learn the keys to success in building your network marketing business—from the man *Success* magazine called a "Millionaire Maker" in their cover story.

With this book YOU will:

- Get the six keys that unlock the door to success in network marketing.
- Learn how to build your business free from doubt and fear.

- Discover how the way you listen has limited your success.
- Accomplish your goals in record time by shifting your listening.
- Use the Zen of Prospecting to draw people to you like a magnet.
- Build rapport and find your prospect's hot buttons instantly.
- Pick the perfect prospecting approach for you.
- Turn any prospect's objection into the very reason they join.
- Identify your most productive prospecting sources.
- Win the numbers game of network marketing.
- Develop a step-by-step business plan that ensures your future.
- Design a Single Daily Action that increases your income 10 times.
- Rate yourself as a top sponsor and business partner.
- Create a passionate vision that guarantees your success.
- And More!!!

10 Weeks to Network Marketing Success:
The Secrets to Launching Your Very Own Million-
Dollar Organization in a 10-Week Business-Building
and Personal-Development Self-Study Course

Learn the business-building and personal-development secrets that will put you squarely on the path to network marketing success. The *10 Weeks to Network Marketing Success* is a powerful course that will grow your business with velocity and change your life!

With this course, YOU will:

- Learn exactly how to set up a powerful 10-week action plan that will propel your business growth.
- Learn how to prospect in your most productive niche markets.
- Discover your most effective pathways to success.
- Learn how to persuasively influence your prospects by listening to contribute value.
- Build your business rapidly by making powerful requests.
- Discover the secret to acting from your commitments.
- Create a powerful life-changing structure for personal development.
- See the growth that comes from evaluating your progress on a regular basis.
- Learn how listening in a new and powerful way will skyrocket your business.
- Uncover the secret to accepting complete responsibility for your business.
- Learn how to transform problems into breakthroughs.
- Develop the charisma that allows you to instantly connect with others on a heart-to-heart level.
- Identify the secrets to stepping into leadership and being the source of your success.
- And much more!

The *10 Weeks to Network-Marketing Success* Program contains 10 weekly exercises on 4 CDs plus a 37-page workbook.

Network Marketing Resources

1. The Center for Personal Reinvention, www.CenterFor PersonalReinvention.com. Books, CDs, coaching, and

courses by Dr. Joe Rubino and Dr. Tom Ventullo to champion your network marketing business and your life. Free newsletter, articles, and success tips.

2. Mach2.org, www.mach2.org. Richard Brooke is one of network marketing's premier visionaries. This site contains articles and wisdom to build your business on a solid foundation.

3. *Networking Times*, www.NetworkingTimes.com. The premier publication in the network marketing industry.

4. The Greatest Networker, www.GreatestNetworker.com. A great generic resource spearheaded by John Milton Fogg, to support network marketing success.

5. Fortune Now, www.FortuneNow.com. Tom "Big Al" Schreiter's web site. Tom is one of the funniest speakers and an overall great guy with lots of knowledge about how to succeed in MLM.

6. PassionFire International, Industry Trainer, www.Passion fire.com. Doug Firebaugh's site, containing great resources to support business-building success.

7. Randy Gage, www.MLMTrainingCentral.com. Randy is one of the foremost trainers in the MLM industry. Great information.

8. *Network Marketing Business Journal*, www.NMBJ.com. A news publication owned by Keith Laggos. Timely news and training articles about the network marketing industry.

9. Brilliant Exchange, www.BrilliantExchange.com. Tim Sales of "Brilliant Compensation" fame's training and resource site.

10. MLM University, www.MLMU.com. Hilton Johnson's site. Articles, tools, and trainings by a top sales–trainer.

11. Cutting Edge Media, www.MyMLMHome.com. Lead Generation.
12. Online Automation, www.ResponsiveLeads.net. Lead Generation.
13. *Home Business* Magazine, www.HomeBusinessMag.com. Working from home articles and resources.

INDEX

Unselfishness, 174–175,
177–178, 194–195
Upline leaders, 26
URL Wire, 103

Value, creating for prospect,
139–142, 162–163
Values (personal), visioning
and, 7–9
Visioning, 1–20
creation of, 5–9
income goals and, 1–5
leadership and, 170
necessary for leadership
role, 192

self-motivation and,
9–12
writing of vision, 12–20
Vollmer, Don and Mary
Lou, 19–20
Vulnerability, 172

Warm market list, *see*
Notification names list
Web site, 25, 111–113. *See
also* Internet
Weekly training meetings,
154–155, 196–197
Writing, of vision, 12–13
samples, 14–20